Reading after ten
Teaching young readers Part 2

Elizabeth Goodacre   John Harris   Colin Harrison
John Foster   Chris Walker
Edited by Chris Longley

BRITISH BROADCASTING CORPORATION

This book accompanies the BBC Radio programme *Reading after ten (Teaching young readers : part 2)*, first broadcast in *Lifelines – work and training* on Radio 3 at 7.00 to 7.30 pm on Tuesdays, starting October 1977.

Published to accompany a series of programmes prepared in consultation with the BBC Further Education Advisory Council

Published by the British Broadcasting Corporation
35, Marylebone High Street, London W1M 4AA.
ISBN 0 563 16177 9
First published 1977
© The authors and the BBC
Printed in England by litho at The Anchor Press Ltd,
and bound by Wm Brendon & Son Ltd, both of Tiptree, Essex.
This book is set in Monotype 10/12pt Old Style No. 2.

Contents

Acknowledgment is due to the following for permission to reproduce material:
E. J. ARNOLD & SON LTD for extracts from *The griffin readers: The fight with the black pirates* by Sheila K. McCullagh (Book 10) *Racing to read: Woodside Farm The old water-mill* by A. E. Tansley & R. H. Nicholis (Book 1); THE AUTHOR PHYLLIS FLOWERDEW, THE EXECUTORS OF THE LATE SIR FRED J. SCHONELL AND THE PUBLISHERS OLIVER & BOYD for extracts from H. V. library book no. 7: *Catch the monkeys*; AUTHOR for extract from *Introduction to biology* by D. G. Mackean published by John Murray Ltd; BASIL BLACKWELL PUBLISHER AND THE SCHOOLS COUNCIL AND ITS RESEARCH AND DEVELOPMENT PROJECT IN COMPENSATORY EDUCATION for extract from *The Swansea test of phonic skills* by Philip Williams; CONTROLLER, HER MAJESTY'S STATIONERY OFFICE for extracts from *A language for life: The Bullock report*; JONATHAN CAPE LTD for extract from *The silver sword* by Ian Serraillier published by William Heinemann Ltd; DR. ELIZABETH GOODACRE for *Hallowe'en night* GEORGE G. HARRAP & CO. LTD for *The Holborn reading scale* by A. F. Watts; HEINEMANN EDUCATIONAL BOOKS LTD for extract from *Ordinary level physics* by Abbott, for extract from *Geography of the British Isles* by Graves and White and for extract from *Focus on rubber* by N. F. Newbury; HOLMES MCDOUGALL LTD for extract from *Scope for reading: Book 3*; LONGMAN GROUP LTD for extract from *Man alone* by J. Mulgan; MILLS & BOON LTD for extract from *A certificate course in practical biology Vol. 2* by J. W. Lee and D. Martin; THOMAS NELSON & SONS LTD for the text from page 3 of *Crime and punishment* by D. Church and B. Ford and The Metropolitan Police for the illustration; PENGUIN EDUCATIONAL BOOKS: CONNECTIONS SERIES for extract from *The lawbreakers* by Ray Jenkins and for extract from *The making of a nation 1603–1789* by A. J. Patrick (History of Britain series); LAURENCE POLLINGER LTD on behalf of the Estate of the late Mrs. Frieda Lawrence for 'Work' from *The complete poems of D. H. Lawrence Vol. 2* published by William Heinemann Ltd; SCOTTISH COUNCIL FOR RESEARCH IN EDUCATION AND HODDER & STOUGHTON LTD for extract from the *Burt word reading test* 1974 revision; SCIENCE RESEARCH ASSOCIATES (CANADA) LTD AND SCIENCE RESEARCH ASSOCIATES (ENGLAND) LTD for extract *Power builder: Silver no. 6* (4 pages) *Rate builder, No. 6 builder* and *A record page* from International Reading Laboratory 2; WARD LOCK EDUCATIONAL LTD for extracts from *Writing and learning across the curriculum* by Nancy Martin: Reprinted by special permission from Flanders *Analyzing teaching behavior 1970* Addison-Wesley, Reading, Mass.; Extracts from pages 17, 18 & 19 of *Language, the learner and the school* (1969) by Douglas Barnes reprinted by permission of Penguin Books Ltd.

The drawings on pages 15 and 16 are by Alan Cracknell.
The photographs on the front cover, pages 6, 26, 4, 9, 82, 104, and 130 were taken by Howard Blakemore, and that on page 114 by C. N. Russell.

Foreword

'In the middle years there should be three major emphases. The first is to consolidate the work of the early years, and to give particular help to those children who for one reason or another have failed to make progress. The second is to maintain and extend the idea of reading as an activity which brings great pleasure and is a personal resource of limitless value. The third is to develop the pupil's reading from the general to the more specialised.'
A language for life, 1975

In his foreword to the BBC publication *Teaching young readers* (Part 1, age 4–9), to which this book is the sequel, **Lord** Bullock remarked that the committee which he had chaired and which reported under the title *A language for life*, 'paid considerable attention to broadcasting as a very important resource for reading and language development in schools. But', he acknowledged, 'apart from noting the opportunities offered by Open University degree and post-experience courses, we are not able to pursue the wider question of the contribution which broadcasting might make to the in-service training of teachers.

I am very glad, therefore', he wrote, 'to learn of the plans BBC Radio has made, through its Further Education Department, to offer two consecutive short courses in 1976 and 1977 for those already concerned in schools with *Teaching young readers*.'

Reading after ten, in conjunction with a series of ten radio programmes, constitutes the second of these two short courses, and is designed particularly for teachers in middle and secondary schools. Like *Teaching young readers* the series has been prepared in consultation with the BBC's Further Education Advisory Council and with teachers and organisers active in this particular field. We hope that it will provide practising teachers with suggestions about ways of organising and developing the reading skills of older children in school so that they may be better able to cope with the reading demands made upon them not only in English classes but across the whole range of the school curriculum.

It is proposed that the programmes of both courses will be re-broadcast on BBC Radio in the winter and spring of 1978–9.

Part 1   Introduction

by Colin Harrison, Lecturer in English in Education,
University of Nottingham School of Education

To many teachers, particularly those in secondary schools, the suggestion that they have a vital role to play in developing children's reading comes as something of a surprise. Yet this is precisely what is suggested in the Bullock report, *A language for life*, and it is the reason why this publication and the radio series related to it have been produced. You may well wonder why such a radical and demanding recommendation was made: surely the overwhelming majority of children are reasonably competent readers by the time they enter secondary school? Furthermore, wouldn't the majority of top junior and secondary teachers claim to be ignorant about the nature of the reading process and ways to develop reading? Insisting that all teachers should accept some responsibility for developing reading thus seems either unrealistic or irresponsible, given the already heavy demands on teachers' time.

The first aim of this introduction, therefore, is to explain why this emphasis on reading development has come about, and the second must be to reassure teachers that they *can* begin to work on reading in their own subject area without having to embark on a major course in theory, and without having to change their syllabus or diminish their course content.

The strongest argument in favour of giving special attention to reading comes from an examination of what we are already asking children to do in secondary school. When you begin to analyse exactly what average children are required to read in order to cope with CSE or 'O' level courses it seems unfair *not* to offer them special help in developing the skills they need. The exercise of looking at what a child is required to read *in every subject* over a single week can be very instructive in making this point.

Look at reading in your own school

You could obtain information similar to that used as the basis for discussion in the following pages. Ask a reliable volunteer (with perhaps a second child as reserve) to record *all* reading in every lesson over one week. At the end of the week you could give details of page references and worksheets to the colleagues who taught each lesson, and ask them to make photocopies and bring them along to a meeting at which you would all read and discuss problems in the *others'* subject area from a non-specialist viewpoint. You could also *compare* the reading of children in different age groups.

If this exercise is done fully it does generate a great deal of information. There is only room here to look at the lessons of one day, rather than a whole week. Nevertheless the activities of the two girls are typical of those in their whole week, and of those in many other schools. Julie and Karen were both rated by their teachers as 'average' readers (that is their chronological age matched their reading age), and as 'CSE grade 2 or 3 potential' in most subjects. They go to a fairly large urban comprehensive school.

In reading through these two diaries you might like to have some questions in mind:

How much reading are the children asked to do?

Are they reading books, worksheets or the blackboard?

How important is specialist vocabulary?

What is the purpose of their reading? (e.g. to seek information, make a summary, carry out a task, or to read for personal pleasure)

Which reading tasks look interesting? Which look potentially boring?

Which passages seem the most readable? Which seem the least readable?

One day's reading for a first-year girl (Julie)

These are Julie's own lesson outlines, and notes on what she had to read, together with samples of the texts:

MONDAY
Periods 1 and 2 English
Read for 20 minutes out of 'Silver Sword' or library books
Then we read story of Odysseus and Circe together
and had to write it in rough for homework.
Reading. I read 'Silver Sword', then Odysseus and Circe

SAMPLE:

ON a bare hillside in the Swiss canton of Appenzell a village was being built. It was an international children's village, the first of its kind in the world. Before the war there was only an old farmhouse there, surrounded by fields with flocks of sheep and herds of cows with tinkling bells. Now the first house, with its broad gables and deep eaves, was already up. Others were going up at top speed. Swiss schoolchildren had collected £30,000 to help pay for the work. A great Swiss youth organization had provided more. Many of the workers gave their help free. Men and boys came from all over Europe. By 1946 Danes, Swedes, Austrians, English, Swiss, Germans and Italians were camping together and working happily side by side. A few months

Period 3 History
We copied notes off the board about Vikings and Danes
from 900-1016. We wrote from notes into best books.
Reading We read about Vikings and Danes off the
board.

SAMPLE:

Let *a* and *b* stand for any two members of the set of counting numbers.
Is it always true that

$$a \times b = b \times a?$$

The use of letters helps us to say something about *all* the members of a
set without listing every single one of them. In this case, they are
'substitutes' or 'stand ins' or 'understudies' for counting numbers.
(Because of this, they can be joined with signs like ' + ' and ' × ' and ' = ' as
though they really were numbers.) They stand for counting numbers until
a particular counting number replaces them.

SAMPLE:

TASK D
1 Find out why fur is such a good insulator.
   Clue: think of a string vest or a cellular blanket.
2 The Eskimos were in constant danger because they could not
   cover up one part of themselves. Which part was it?
   Clue: cornea.

The Eskimo still has to rely upon his dogs for travelling. The husky
dogs are powerful animals often nearly savage, which work in
teams of four to seven behind a leader dog. This is another reason
why the Eskimo has to be a good hunter, for he has to feed these
animals large quantities of meat each day. The long sledge, made
of wood with metal runners, may have raised canvas sides in winter
to provide some protection from the wind. In good conditions the
team averages more than 35 km a day and has been known to reach
up to 160 km.

Map

When we look at a map of the polar areas on a polar projection (see Figure 67) and contrast it with the more familiar Mercator projection, it seems a new view of the world.

Today, maps like this are used by the navigators of aircraft flying across the pole from Europe to Asia, say from London to Tokyo.

Periods 7 and 8 Science.
We did worksheets and experiments with different amounts of heat.
Reading We had to read the worksheets to see what to do.

SAMPLE:

Instructions

(1) Measure out 10cm^3 of sodium thiosulphate solution into a conical flask and add 40cm^3 of distilled water. The temperature needed is about 20 C, so warm gently if necessary.

(2) Remove the heat, add 5cm^3 of 2M hydrochloric acid, note the temperature and time and gently shake the mixture.

(3) As in the previous experiment, judge the density of the precipitate by viewing a cross on a piece of paper through it.

(4) Enter the time in the table of results below.

(5) Repeat, using the same quantities of thiosulphate solution, distilled water and acid, and the same procedure as above, only first at 30 C, then again at 40 C, then at 50 C and finally at 60 C.

One day's reading for a fourth-year girl (Karen)

As Julie did, Karen gave us her outline of the lessons. Because of absence, some of her work involves catching up what had been missed.

Monday
Periods 1-2 Physics
Copied up notes on engines, jets, rockets out of O'level Physics book. Weighed Objects and did a table.
Reading: Read work in book about engines, jets and rockets. Read table off blackboard.

SAMPLE:

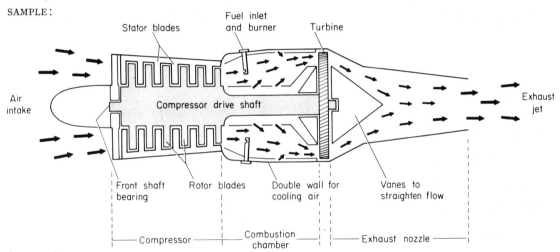

Jet engines

An aircraft jet engine works on the same principle as a rocket, the difference between them is concerned only with the method of obtaining the high-velocity gas jet. Fig. 71 shows, in simplified form, the construction of an axial-flow gas turbine or jet engine. The fuel used in these engines is kerosene (paraffin). This is sprayed through burners into combustion chambers, where it burns in a blast of compressed air and produces a high-velocity jet of gas which emerges from the exhaust nozzle.

The air supply is drawn in at the front of the engine and compressed by a turbine compressor. A turbine is simply a special kind of fan having alternate sets of fixed and rotating metal blades. The compressor itself is driven by another smaller turbine worked by the exhaust jet.

> Period 3 Physical
> Played tiggy and basketball.
>
> Period 4 Mathematics
> Did school maths project Book X, Page 35 no 4
> Reading: Read question no. 4.

SAMPLE:

In an athletics test involving 70 pupils, standards were awarded as follows: sprinting 31, jumping 29, throwing 16, sprinting and throwing 12, all three events 5, jumping only 7, throwing only 15. Define suitable sets B, S, J and T and represent the given information on a Venn diagram.

State (i) the number of pupils gaining sprinting standards only, (ii) the number of pupils gaining standards in exactly two events, (iii) the number of pupils who did not gain any standards.

> Period 5 Geography
> Answered questions on town planning.
> Reading: Read questions on page 80 of Graves and white. Got answers from the book.

SAMPLE:

6. Explain why apparently quite serviceable buildings are demolished in city centres.

7. Give at least two reasons why the unplanned development or redevelopment of towns would probably be unwise in the 20th century.

8. (a) What British Act of Parliament makes local authorities responsible for planning the development of the areas under their control?

   (b) In the case of Birmingham, (i) what steps did the planning authority take to get an approved development plan, and (ii) what were the main aims of the plan?

9. Supposing you were responsible for redeveloping a block of land for industry, shops and private dwellings, what offices would you have to consult to ensure that proper services were provided?

Period 6. English
Looked at, and talked about 'The Unknown Citizen'
and 'Work. Began own Poem on Machinery.
Reading. Poems by Auden and D.H. Lawrence.

SAMPLE:

WORK

There is no point in work
unless it absorbs you
like an absorbing game.

If it doesn't absorb you
if it's never any fun,
don't do it.

When a man goes out into his work
he is alive like a tree in spring,
he is living, not merely working.

When the Hindus weave thin wool into long, long lengths
    of stuff
with their thin dark hands and their wide dark eyes and
    their still souls absorbed
they are like slender trees putting forth leaves, a long white
    web of living leaf,
the tissue they weave,
and they clothe themselves in white as a tree clothes itself
    in its own foliage.

Periods 7-8 Biology.
Wrote some dictated notes in rough about the heart.
Drew diagrams. Began essay on the heart.
Reading. Diagrams and description of the heart.

The heart

The heart is a muscular pumping organ. It is thought that it has evolved from the highly muscular region of an artery. It is divided into four chambers; the left and right sides do not communicate. The upper chambers, the *atria*, which are relatively thin-walled, receive blood from the veins (Fig. 19.8). Oxygenated blood from the lungs enters the *left atrium* via the *pulmonary vein* and deoxygenated blood from the body enters the *right atrium* from the *venae cavae* (Fig. 19.9). Relaxation of the ventricular muscle allows the ventricles to expand and fill with blood which flows in from the atria and veins (Fig. 19.10). Simultaneous contraction of both atria forces the blood they contain into the corresponding ventricles and, about 0·1 sec. later, the ventricles contract simultaneously, expelling their blood into the arteries and round the body. Both ventricles have thick muscular walls but those of the left are thicker, having to pump blood all round the entire body via the *aorta*. The *right ventricle* pumps blood to the lungs through the *pulmonary artery*.

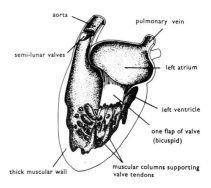

Fig. 19.8 The heart cut open (This diagram is very much reduced and the two other diagrams mentioned in the text are not reproduced here).

The Schools Council *Effective use of reading* project team did a similar exercise to this on an in-service course, and discussed the results with groups of teachers. Many of the teachers felt shocked and horrified: they had forgotten just how much we ask of fourth-year children. As adults, we try to keep clear of highly technical writing in a subject which is unfamiliar to us, and when we are forced to give attention to a document written in a specialised language (such as a legal contract) we rely heavily on an expert to tell us what it means. When you look at these two groups of passages what strikes you at once is that Karen, the fourth-year pupil, is grappling with what seem to be five different languages, each with its own vocabulary difficulties and constructions. The reading skills needed for dealing with these texts also differ.

Karen's Monday begins with Physics, and a high-level reading comprehension task: in catching up work she has missed through absence Karen has to try to explain how a jet engine works. But the conceptual level of the problem is only one of her difficulties. There are others related to how the text is written. What does the author mean by 'to impart an initial rotation'? How many 'O' level candidates could gloss this as 'to start it turning'? You might also wonder how many would be happy with 'propel', 'drawn in' meaning 'sucked in', and 'ignite'. It is extremely difficult for a non-specialist to raise the question of how crucial a scientifically precise term is to the accuracy of the text, but you can be sure that if the passage contains constructions which are totally unfamiliar, they will cause the reader almost as much difficulty as if they were in a foreign language examination. The reading task, then, is to *produce a summary* which demonstrates an understanding of how a turbine and the fuel come to produce jet propulsion.

By contrast, the reading in Karen's Maths lesson seems comparatively simple, although someone who could cope with set theory and Venn diagrams but who did not understand what standards were in athletics might find the question difficult. There might also be a problem for some readers in interpreting instructions 'define suitable sets' or 'represent the given information on. . . .' There has recently been a good deal of debate about whether 'new maths' textbooks are too demanding in terms of verbal content. Some courses have been attacked as being much too condensed and full of specialised terminology for the average child (and some teachers!) to be able to cope with them. Certainly a question such as 'Do these tetrominoes tesselate?' would frighten most of us, and this is in fact to be found in the most popular junior school Maths course, not a secondary one.

● Ask a *group of children* to go through a chapter of a textbook you use and to make a list of any words they don't know. Any word which is noted more than twice can be included in a *glossary* which you then make out, and *hang up* for reference in your classroom or laboratory.

What, briefly, are the other reading tasks Karen has to tackle after lunch?

In Geography, finding the answers to those questions on town planning requires a good deal of skill in *finding and marshalling information*. She needs to read, sift, select, reject, and finally summarise what she has read for questions 6–8, and to rework the evidence which is in the text in order to answer question 9.

In English, the first six lines of Lawrence's poem *Work* seem a slightly ironic comment on the rest of the day. It is difficult to believe that Karen would find herself absorbed in every one of her eight lessons. This reading task seems rather out of phase with the other parts of her day, in that a full response to the poem requires a probing for ambiguity and a tolerance of uncertainty which would perhaps be unprofitable in other subjects. Another way of describing the reading in English might be to say that with a

poem you are looking for *meanings*, while in other subjects you are looking for *meaning*. This is a crucial difference.

In Biology, Karen's textbook extract offers strong support to the widely held view that this subject is the most difficult of all in terms of specialist vocabulary. Even setting aside for the moment the italicised names for parts of the heart, the reader still has to grapple with 'organ', 'chambers', 'deoxygenated', 'passive flow', and 'contraction'. The accompanying diagram helps, in that the various parts of the heart are labelled, but they still may be difficult to read. To a child they may appear more like foreign placenames on a map than words which have any meaning, and there is a sense in which this is so. The word 'aorta' is a label, just like the placename 'Linköping' is a label; however well Karen can visualise the functions of the heart, she will still need to learn the word 'aorta' and a good many others, since knowing them is an important shorthand form of reference. The point is that it is harder to learn words which only serve as *labels*, compared with words such as 'density', 'volume', and 'mass' which are closely linked as *concepts*.

Incidentally, in talking to an author of a biology textbook, I was reminded of the teacher's responsibility not only towards their children and their reading but also the material itself. He remarked, 'HMIs and colleagues have told me I might be disconcerted to see how textbooks are used in some schools. A textbook is a resource, to be used not in isolation but in conjunction with carefully programmed teaching.'

You may like to consider the words in the glossary of a textbook (or in one you have compiled yourself from children's suggestions), and split them up into labels and concepts. Do you feel you already introduce these to children in different ways? If so, how?

Do the concepts form a hierarchy? If so, how are they related? Do you introduce them to children in a way that demonstrates this relationship? Do you introduce labels with a visual aid? Always? If you do not they may be much more difficult for the reader to cope with.

So far we have looked closely at the reading of Karen, the fourth-year girl. But what about Julie, in the first year? The fourth-year reading is very demanding in many ways, and it seems useful to ask how the demands at first-form level differ from those in the fourth year.

In English, Julie's class reader is *The silver sword*. The brief extract reproduced is from the final part of the book, and although it contains one or two difficult words ('canton', 'gables', 'eaves') you would probably expect most children to be able to cope, since not knowing them would be unlikely to hold up progress in reading the story.

In History, no book or worksheet was used at all. The teacher's aims were to convey information about the vikings, and *if language skills are being developed it is perhaps in the area of writing that this is being done.* The child's task is to turn the teacher's own notes into prose.

In Mathematics, two phrases stand out as potentially difficult, the construction 'Let a and b stand for . . .' and 'counting numbers'. A first-year child coming across this rare subjunctive may well feel 'why not? Who's stopping them?' if he or she glosses 'let' as 'don't stop'. Similarly, 'counting numbers' may take on strange meanings if the child reads 'counting' as a verb rather than part of a noun phrase. This short passage reminds us how difficult it is for subject specialists to represent their content in a rigorous and consistent way, while still using reasonably familiar language. As you will see in the section below on the reading process, unfamiliar language structures are just as great a problem for the reader as unfamiliar words. For Julie, then, her reading in Mathematics requires her *to come to terms with unfamiliar constructions*, and if she is to be able to work from the book on her own (as she must for homework) she must be helped by her teacher to do this. If the teaching in class only covers the course *content*, then she may eventually become one of those unfortunate children who can do the mathematical operations, but can't comprehend a CSE examination question.

In Geography, the notes Julie made only partly cover the reading she had to do. Presumably *in order to complete Task D she needed to do some 'research' of her own, using a number of possible resources: a dictionary, an encyclopaedia, another general reference book, or of course her neighbour.* You can see in these activities skills being demanded which will be most valuable in later years. It is important, though, that you remember that only by being vigilant will you be able to test whether a girl like Julie is beginning to develop such skills, or is simply asking a brighter neighbour for the information she needs.

In Science, Julie's reading task is *to interpret instructions for conducting an experiment*, and although the instructions are broken up into stages, there are nevertheless some parts of the worksheet which might lead you to think that science teachers don't write prose which is any simpler than that in science textbooks. 'Judge the density of the precipitate' is one example, and the final sentence is another. In this, the teacher manages to attach a thirty-two-word group of subordinate clauses to a one-word main clause. 'Repeat, using the same quantities of thiosulphate solution, distilled water and acid, and the same procedure as above, only first at 30°C, then again at 40°C, then at 50°C and finally at 60°C.' This remarkable sentence will put a tremendous load on the memory of the child who is reading it, and it could have been expressed far more comprehensibly if it had been broken up into two sentences.

Worksheets are important in many subjects, and yet we rarely have the time to evaluate them. The crucial question, when a child is unable to carry on with a worksheet, is this: *is the worksheet content too difficult, or is the child having problems because of the way in which the worksheet is written or printed?*

Worksheet workshop
arrange to sit in on a colleague's lesson in your own subject. Look and listen. *At what points do children get stuck? What do they do about it? Does your harrassed colleague have to give in and* explain *what they have to do thus* bypassing *the need for the children to read and think it out for themselves?*

Don't forget there may be some children whom you regard as non-readers who are *readers in other lessons! Ask a child to read the worksheet quietly to you.*

Watch out for
– children unable to pronounce *difficult words; they may be way out of their depth*
– children who 'read' words which aren't there; what they are conveying to you is what they are expecting *to read, as opposed to what the author has put. These parts might be ripe for rewriting.*

Arrange a 'worksheet across the curriculum' group, at which different departments all bring sample worksheets for discussion. You could even invite some children *to join the group – after all, they are the consumers. Which worksheets are most illegible? Which seem most attractive? Which seem most difficult? How can they be improved?*

WARNING *– the English department may be in for a shock!*

Get together a consortium *to produce the Six Million Dollar Worksheet!*

In deciding whether a book or worksheet has a level of prose difficulty which is too great for the average child, we tend to rely on personal judgments.

What might be useful would be a means of estimating the difficulty level of texts in an objective and reasonably reliable way, so that we could feel that we were not relying solely on our own intuitive judgments. There are ways of estimating difficulty using readability formulae, and these can give you a *reading level* which is the age at which you would expect that the average child could cope with the passage in question. Most formulae work from measuring such aspects of the text as average sentence length and the proportion of long words in the passage. The use of readability formulae is discussed more fully in Part 4 of this book, *Resources for reading* (page 100) but to give you an idea of the sort of information they provide, this table gives the reading levels (based on Flesch grade score) of the texts in the girls' diaries.

Julie (1st yr)	11·7	Karen (4th yr)	14·7
English	11·7	English	*
Mathematics	12·5	Mathematics	18·8
Geography	12·3	Geography	19·5
Science	15·8	Physics	16·00
formula invalid		Biology	14·9

It's interesting to note that it is in English – which is the only subject where at present you might hope to find a reading specialist – that we find the *easiest* passage. The readability formula suggests that the first-year Maths and Geography texts are not too difficult, but that the science worksheet is written at about fourth- or fifth-year level in terms of its prose difficulty.

No figure is given for the poem Karen had to read: most readability formulae are derived from an analysis of the difficulty levels of expository prose, and so it would be invalid to apply a formula to them. All the other samples of Karen's reading (and these were not specially selected to prove the point) are rated as difficult, with the passage from her Geography book being rated as above nineteen years. It's sobering to think that the passage gives a series of instructions, and seems uncomfortably similar to an 'O' level examination question in terms of vocabulary and style. No wonder some teachers have serious worries about children who know their subject but cannot cope with the examination paper.

Other teachers of CSE and 'O' level groups bemoan the fact that their children cannot cope at all with the reading demands of their subject, and when you look at the reading of children in some lower secondary classes you might begin to wonder whether enough is done to prepare for these heavy demands. In general terms you would expect to find less emphasis on reading in the first form than the fourth, because of the value of practical activities and talk as ways into new work and ideas. However, in some schools, so many individual departments have gone over to worksheets that there is a serious danger that reading skills which have been initially fostered in junior school will not be developed. Economic stringencies have forced many departments to channel their resources towards examination classes, and a teacher may decide that the first form will have to do without a textbook without realising that others have done the same.

The Schools Council *Effective use of reading* project team recorded the reading of a first-year child over a whole week in one comprehensive school, and noted the use of printed books in only three subjects, English, French and Maths. In Music, History, RE, Art, Geography, Science,

Games and Needlework, the only reading was from teachers' notes on the blackboard, or (more rarely) from a worksheet.

It looks therefore as if it can be extremely useful to keep a systematic record of what reading skills we are requiring of children, and whether children are gradually developing those they need. The *reading cheklist* is a framework within which you can record this information. As you can see at once, the checklist is not concerned with basic aspects of reading, such as pronunciation or word recognition – it looks at what children can *do* with their reading.

Reading checklist

1 Comprehension

● Can child retell main facts of story/passage – in his (or her) own words?

● Can child retell main facts of story/passage – in correct order?

● Can child summarise story/passage
 – with texts?   – without texts?
 – orally?   – in writing?

● Can child predict outcome of story (and defend decision by referring to the text)?

● Can child frame his or her own questions on a text (for example, construct and mark a comprehension test on it)?

● Can pupil work *independently* from a work-sheet?

2 Varying how you read

● Does pupil always tend to read at only one speed?

● Does child *skim* when appropriate? (i.e. read quickly for general impression)

● Does child *scan* when appropriate? (i.e. read quickly to find a particular word or phrase)

● Does the pupil tend to read information books from page 1 *regardless of purpose*?

3 Finding information

● Can child select a book for work on a topic?

● Can he reject a book which is
 – too difficult?
 – inappropriate?

● Can he use a dictionary
 – at all?   – to good effect?

● Can he use (*does* he use)
 – contents page?   – appendix?
 – sub-headings?   – glossary?
 – index?
 – figures or charts to good effect?

● Can he find encyclopaedia articles
(for example on
 – King George II   – Early Rome
 – Greek temples)
(i.e. does he go beyond simple alphabetical clues?)

There are other examples of reading checklists in Part 2, page 74.

In the *comprehension* section of the checklist, the fifth question, 'Can the child frame his or her own questions on a text?', is perhaps the crucial one, which will give you most insight into how much a reader is comprehending. The phrase 'active interrogation of a text' from the Bullock report is focussing on precisely the same aspect of reading. Comprehension is related to the ability (and willingness) of the reader to *reflect* on what has been read, and if this seems a banal definition it perhaps demonstrates the current tentative-ness which some psychologists have about opting for any more specific definition.

Comprehension is nothing if it is not *personal*, and although the other subsections are important in many school subjects, and are well worth monitoring, there is a sense in which they are all implied by the fifth. By asking his *own* questions, the reader is able to begin from his own experience, and to set that of the author against his own. This is what fluent readers do all the time, but it is very different from an arbitrary comprehension task, such as defining hard words or rewriting facts.

The ability to obtain and use evidence is often one of the most crucial skills a child needs to possess at CSE or 'O' level and beyond, and it can only be done well if the reader *varies* his approach to reading at different stages of the task. Amazing as it may seem, some sixth-formers will approach a reading 'research' task with only one strategy – they begin at word 1 and go on reading to word 50,000. This second section gives you some headings for looking at whether your children do this or not. The crucial question is not whether they *can* vary their reading, but whether they *do*. You may need to spend much more time *motivating* a child to think about the best way to find certain information than you would in teaching the difference between skimming and scanning. The key word here is the final one, *purpose*.

Right from the start you can begin to stress to children that their *purpose* for reading should determine how they approach a book. In the third part the first two subsections of the checklist on selecting and rejecting a book might well involve the reader in framing his own questions, and in reading in different ways in order to discover whether a book is suitable for his purpose or not. *Rejecting a book is a higher level skill than selecting one,* and at first-year secondary level it is a useful idea to try to assess every child on their ability to do both.

Selecting or rejecting a book:
Give a child a topic (e.g. 'rabies') and follow

him round the library. Log what he does, and then see if you can find any information he missed, or whether he opted for any irrelevant material. Discuss your own and the child's approach with him.

Give a group a Jackdaw *of a dozen or so pieces of evidence for a topic, at least two of which are really irrelevant. Prepare a plan for an essay, then discuss as a group how you set about it and criteria for selection of evidence.*

An important question for you as a teacher is: do the abilities referred to in the checklist develop spontaneously, or do they need to be taught? It is generally felt that in about the top 10 per cent of readers most of these skills develop as readers see adults using them. The other 90 per cent need to be taught. Of course, most teachers are in this top 10 per cent, and therefore tend not to realise the problems of the others, or at least they take a little time to become aware of those problems.

One approach to developing your own sensitivity, and the children's reading skills, would be to:

Use the checklist to decide:
– what skills are necessary in your subject
– which of these skills the children have mastered

Make a special effort to introduce those in which specific children need help.

Try to ensure that the children are reading for some purpose, *and not doing skills training simply as an exercise, otherwise there may not be transfer of the skill practised in isolation when the child needs it.*

Part 2 of this book contains a variety of other ways to develop skills like these identified in the checklist.

The reading process –
in a competent reader

In a book which aims to be firmly practical, it is reasonable to begin with some examples of typical reading tasks which children are set, followed by suggestions for activities which will allow you to compare the picture which emerges from your own school with the one offered here. This is important, because by doing the activities you will come to have a clearer understanding of the kind of issue raised so far. Also, the information you obtain will have been determined by that unique blend of problems which relate to your own school, and this will be a more valuable starting point than a more general description.

However, we have reached the point at which it is going to be necessary to inject a little theory, and to describe in a general way the nature of the reading process. You may already have wondered what exactly a reader does when he reads a passage. In the previous section we referred to the need for a reader to vary the rate at which he reads, according to the task in hand. For example, if a child wants to know whether a particular history book has any relevant information for a worksheet on mediaeval clothing, he may take a book from the library shelf and read it in the following way (you might like to try doing this yourself):

1 Flicks through pages, starting from end of book (hardly time to read anything except the occasional word).

2 Reads lists of contents (reading is very swift; perhaps looks for a few key words or phrases).

3 Skims over first few pages of a chapter (noting headings, occasional phrases).

4 Notes relevant sub-headings, reads whole section (much slower, reflective, thoughtful reading).

You may wonder whether the reading process is essentially the same in each of these activities, and the issue is by no means a barren theoretical one – it has crucial implications for how we should help remedial readers, and it helps to explain why our children are taught to read as they are. So how does a competent reader read? When we read quickly are we simply speeding up the process, and doing the same things as usual, only faster? The short answer is 'No', and the example on the next page helps to explain what happens.

When you read a text of average difficulty you probably fixate about four or five points on every line, and the area of clear vision is no greater than a 10p piece around each of these points. Your brain then does a phenomenal juggling act, not with whole single words as such, but with the *partial* information it is receiving, and the chunks of partial information are matched with familiar grammatical structures and meanings to create a *probable* meaning. If this probable meaning seems sensible no back-tracking is done, and the eye goes on through the text. The key points of the process, then, are:

1 The eye sends the brain *partial* information.

2 The reader makes predictions about *probable* meanings.

3 He matches them with previous knowledge and familiar language patterns.

4 If there is no nonsense, or incompatibility with meanings so far, the process continues.

5 If there is a problem, the eye goes back for *more* information.

This is a highly simplified account of what is now the generally accepted view of the reading process. Professor Kenneth Goodman in the USA

Below: reading at three speeds
1 Too slow – wobbling and about to fall off
2 He's happy – just moving along nicely
3 Too fast – frightened to death, racing like
fury, can't see where he's going

The beginning of the rubber industry

Rubber was one of the strange new plants discovered by Christopher Columbus during his explorations in the New World. One day he saw some village children throwing a small round object to each other. When one of the children dropped it, it did not stay on the ground, but bounced up again into his hands.

Columbus asked what this toy was made of. He was taken to see a tree which had sticky liquid dripping from a gash in its trunk. The children rolled this sticky substance into a ball to make their toy.

Raw rubber taken straight from the tree soon becomes hard and useless. So for many years after the time of Columbus, rubber trees continued to grow wild and no one bothered to cultivate them. Then men discovered a way of making rubber much more useful. You will read about their discoveries on page 23. The demand for raw rubber grew very fast and soon more was needed than could be collected from wild trees in the Brazilian jungle. One man, called Henry Wickham, saw a way of growing more rubber for the world. The story of how he began the modern rubber industry is fascinating.

In 1876, Wickham collected 70,000 seeds from the Brazilian tree which gave the best rubber. He carefully dried and packed the seeds between dried banana leaves. Then he took them to Kew Botanic Gardens in England. There 3,000 of these seeds were successfully grown in the hot houses. The small rubber seedlings were sent to Ceylon and to Malaya. From the seeds collected by Henry Wickham in Brazil have grown the huge rubber plantations in South-East Asia.

has aptly called it a 'psycho-linguistic guessing game', because of the emphasis on using partial information. This account, while it leaves a good deal unsaid about exactly *what* partial information is used, and how it is integrated, is nevertheless rather more satisfactory than the previously held view, which is that we read every word and process it letter by letter, turning the letters into sounds as we go. This does describe what most of us did when *learning* to read, when we were beginning to learn sound–letter relationships, but it doesn't hold water as a description of the process of fluent reading. The only time most of us revert to letter-by-letter processing and 'sounding out' is when we come up against an unfamiliar word, such as 'paregoric'. For this word we might make two or three attempts at pronunciation 'in our heads', and fixate it as many as a dozen times.

It is the fact that normal reading is a kind of high-speed guessing game which explains why we find it difficult to proof-read. The reading process is incredibly flexible, and can cope with all kinds of wrong information such as reversed letters, misprints, punctuation errors and changes in type font, any of which would completely fox a computer. But so long as sense is coming over, the eye bounds on. What does hold up the process are unfamiliar language constructions, so *a when of juggled the about are all sentence words*, the brain gets into an awful state trying to reconcile a sensible anticipated message and the nonsensical message which was actually received.

There are at least two important educational implications from all this. Firstly, we must *expect* children to have difficulty in reading texts in which the language structures are unfamiliar. Infant teachers recognise this and it is why many children actually begin learning to read on a book which they have written themselves, and which the teacher has transcribed from a tape recording of the child's own speech. This approach can also be used to good effect in the secondary school with remedial readers. In primary schools it is usually called the *language experience* approach, and this relates to our point about reading. It is easier for a child to read language which he has experienced before. You must not think this is a call for a conversational prose style to invade all school textbooks; it is more a plea for a greater understanding of what Julie and Karen and their friends are coping with in some of their textbooks and other school reading. (For more information on the language experience approach, see page 47.)

The second implication relates to what you do as a reader when you are faced with a difficult sentence, such as this, out of Karen's physics book:

'In either case, a chemical reaction takes place inside the rocket and creates a large force which propels the gaseous products of combustion out through the tail nozzle with tremendous velocity.'

We have already noted that the reading process is a *cumulative* one, in which partial meanings are built up as the eye sends successive messages to the brain. Now, if you are a fifteen-year-old, and bemused by the phrase 'gaseous products of combustion', the temptation may be to home in on the words of the phrase until you are mesmerised by them, and you despair of understanding the rocket engine. In the event, reading the difficult part very slowly is *not* going to help. It doesn't allow you to build up a clear enough partial picture to permit an overall meaning to emerge. What you need to do, in Eric Lunzer's words, is to 'read fast; think slow'.

There are in fact two distinct kinds of failure to comprehend, one related to reading too slowly, and the other related to reading fast but failing to reflect on what is read. The first extreme is represented in the illustration by the cyclist who is travelling so slowly that he is wobbling all over, and indeed seems about to fall off. He represents the slow reader who is unable to gain enough momentum in his reading to progress. The rather smug cyclist in the middle is travelling at a steady pace, and so is able to take in

Below: these are the first six fixations of a fluent reader who was given the question, 'What is this passage about?' The small circle is the point of each successive fixation and the large circle gives a rough idea of the area which is in focus.

what is going on about him. The harum-scarum sprinter, on the other hand, represents a type of reader you probably know quite well. He is in such a hurry that he has no idea of where he's going, and precious little about where he's been.

These are two points to note about the speed merchant as a reader. Firstly, there is no intrinsic merit in speed reading – broadly speaking, if you double your speed you will comprehend in less detail what you have read. Secondly, you may not allow yourself time to consider *whether* you have understood what you read or not. *What is much more important than speed in reading is flexibility, that is, adjusting the rate of your reading to the task in hand and the difficulty level of the material you are reading.* If the cycling image can sustain it, we could say that a three-speed gearing is more important than a set of lightweight racing equipment.

As a teacher, you are doing more than teaching a subject, you are preparing children for life, and the area of reading skills is one which is universally acknowledged as crucial in relation to employment. If reading skills are to

be fostered, this must be done within the context of a systematic programme of development, and with purposeful reading tasks. But important though the skills are, they are not your only concern. Look at the two lists of personal reading on the next page, contributed at the end of their week of recording by Julie and Karen.

These lists answer the question 'What reading did you do during the week that was not set by the school?' (This includes magazines, comics, newspapers, books.) The top list is from Julie (first year) and the bottom one from Karen (fourth year).
The barrenness of Karen's private reading world may have given you a depressing reminder of how much there is to be done in the area of developing reading for personal enjoyment and enrichment. In our enthusiasm for giving sorely needed attention to the utilitarian side of reading, let us not forget that our work on the aesthetic side remains a primary concern, and that its needs are no less urgent for being less widely advertised.

MONDAY I read 'The Star' (our local paper) and three chapters of my own book called 'On the banks of Plum Creek'.

TUESDAY I read 'The Star' and two chapters of 'On the banks of Plum Creek' and I also read the whole of 'Weekend'.

WEDNESDAY I read 'The Star' and 'The Wizzerchips' comic then four chapters of 'On the banks of Plum Creek' and then I read my own book of horses and ponies.

THURSDAY I read the last two chapters of 'On the banks of Plum Creek' and I read one chapter of 'My friend Flicka' and I read all of 'The Sun' and parts of 'The Star'.

FRIDAY I read 'My friend Flicka'.

Monday.
'Sunday Mirror' and Monday night's 'Star'.

Tuesday
Read Tuesday night's 'Star'.

Wednesday
None.

Thursday and Friday
None.

Reading for enjoyment and enrichment:
Do you know *how much the children you teach*
read in their spare time? If not, you could find
out by giving each child a small Book Review
Notebook *in which to record and report on school*
and private reading, including *non-fiction.*

Does your mark book *for English only contain*
a list of grades or marks? How about keeping a
record of what your children have read? This
will tell you a great deal about their overall
approach to reading, and what is likely to go
down well in class.

● Children take most notice of *each other's*
opinions about which books are worth reading.
You could organise a regular *recommendation*
session in which children report (in small groups
of five or six) on a book they have enjoyed.

● Has your school got a *school bookshop*? You
can set one up very easily. All you need are four
volunteers and a lockable book cupboard (the
ones on castors are best, these can be put in a
prominent place at lunchtimes and then pushed
out of the way). *You may be able to obtain books*
on sale or return from a local bookshop.

Part 2   Teaching and learning
*by Christopher Walker, Senior Lecturer in Reading Development
at City of Manchester College of Education*

The backward reader

The official designation 'backward readers' refers to those whose reading age is two years below their chronological age. For the purposes of this book 'failing' readers are those with reading ages below nine. There is also another category, the 'apparently failing' reader, who in reality is not failing at all but is a slow learner.

The slow learner

He only appears to be failing because his rate of progress is exceptionally slow and the difference between his reading age and his actual age is often much more than two years. Obviously he is backward, but as he can be seen, over a long period of time, to be making steady, though slow, progress he is certainly not failing. His slow progress in reading skill generally stems from one of two causes, though often both operate simultaneously. These are

low IQ
slow developmental pattern.

The IQ range in which slow learners officially fall is within the band 70 to 85 points. The more closely the IQ approaches 70 the more will reading be a difficult task and it would be rare for children to make much progress if their IQ were less than 75 unless they were well adjusted socially and emotionally. Children with IQ below 75 are rarely to be found in ordinary schools and at some stage will have been ascertained as more suitable for special education.

The effect of low IQ on reading growth can be seen in the following case. Johnny is ten years old, but he has a mental age of only seven. That he has an IQ of 70 can be calculated thus:

$$IQ = \frac{\text{mental age}}{\text{chronological age}} \times 100 = \frac{7}{10} \times 100 = 70.$$

This means that at ten, although he has been in school five years, he will only be at the level of general maturity and educability of an *average* child half-way through the last year of infant school.

On the other hand slow progress in reading may be not so much due to 'lack of brains', which is one way of paraphrasing 'low IQ', as to general slowness of developmental pattern. At the moment of conception we inherit through the genes of our parents certain characteristics which under the peculiar environmental influences which affect us make us the unique persons that we are. We also inherit from that moment of conception a timing mechanism which dictates that we shall grow at such and such a rate. Though this rate may be accelerated or retarded by environmental factors there is great divergence between the fastest and slowest possible rates of growth. An easily observable difference in growth rates is that between boys and girls. The latter, on average, develop bone structure, teeth, physical strength and coordination far sooner than boys. These acquisitions enable girls generally to speak, read and write sooner than boys. In the heyday of the eleven-plus the girls' scores had to be adversely weighted, or comparatively few boys would have gone to grammar school.

However, even within the sexes no two persons develop at the same rate. Some children, though they go through all the stages of growth in the normal order, take much longer to reach them. The child who utters his first word at twelve months is likely to be slow in learning to read.

Teaching the slow learner

Assessment

In the first place, you, the teacher of the child between ten and sixteen years old, can best help the slow learner by recognising him for what he is. You will ascertain this by using more than one measuring device. A reading age alone will merely indicate that he is probably backward in reading and by so many years. Some measure of intelligence is also necessary to indicate that he is truly a slow learner and not a child of some ability and potential who is more properly in need of remedial treatment. It is necessary to define clearly the nature of the problem for the slow learner requires quite different treatment from that suitable for remedial cases. Other information, such as records of reading schemes used, books read, approaches tried, particular reading strengths and weaknesses, hobbies and interests, would obviously help you in drawing up a suitable programme.

Teaching principles

Once you know you have a slow learner to deal with the main thing is to go slowly. Slow learners can only learn a bit at a time. They put so much effort into learning each little bit that they soon tire and their concentration flags. By working with them you will soon learn how much to attempt at one go. When they have had enough, stop and give them a complete change of activity. The 'method' then is to work in short bursts, one step at a time, with each step done thoroughly so that they can then tackle the next with confidence. Praise and encouragement help but the best support is the self-confidence that comes from the success of learning each step well. Though working in 'short bursts', don't just fit these in whenever you have a few minutes to spare. Plan well ahead so that the short bursts are regularly spaced and time-tabled. Better ten minutes twice a day, say morning and afternoon, than a whole afternoon just once a week.

Don't be put off teaching the slow learner by your own lack of expertise or by the fact that you were never trained to teach reading. You will only learn to teach reading by teaching

reading. At this moment thousands of adult illiterates are being taught to read by clerks, typists, housewives and pensioners – and being taught successfully. You have the advantage that you are a trained teacher. You will soon find out what your pupil needs and then, whatever you do, do it as well as you can. Your methods may be unorthodox. That doesn't matter – there are as many methods of teaching reading as there are reading teachers. As all known methods of teaching reading have been successful, it is obviously teachers, not methods, that matter. In my experience, the teacher's determination to succeed is the best guarantee of the pupil's success.

A major problem in teaching slow-learning ten- to sixteen-year-olds is finding the right material. Though they may well be only top infants or lower juniors by mental age, physically and socially they are near-adults. They require the carefully graded programme that is built into the typical infant reading scheme, where new words are introduced very few at a time and where there is the reinforcement of frequent repetition. They also need the stimulus of being able to identify with the content, characters and situations developed in the scheme. This is why in fact reading schemes geared to the interest of five- to seven-year-olds are useless for the older slow learners.

Some useful materials for slow learners

Racing to read and *Sound sense*
If you have a slow learner between ten and twelve years old who is also socially very immature, you could try *Racing to read*. The content is not infantile and the vocabulary is carefully controlled with massive repetition. This scheme is also well backed with the *Sound sense* books. These provide excellent supporting activities by means of well-graded written exercises developing phonic work and simple

We walk and walk and come to a river.
A man is sitting by the river catching fish.
He has his net by his side.
The fisherman's little boy is fishing with a little net.

49

Read these sentences.

I had a birthday <u>cake</u>.
I like a <u>game</u> of football.
I was <u>late</u> for school.
The girl's <u>name</u> was Mary.
He ran a good <u>race</u>.

Look at the underlined words again.
What sound does the <u>a</u> make? All the
underlined words are in a family.

Here are some more words in the same
family:

take wave page ate came case gate gave
lake made make same shape shake save.

Now look at these words: <u>a</u>n <u>a</u>nd h<u>a</u>t
b<u>a</u>g P<u>a</u>t m<u>a</u>n f<u>a</u>t.

What sound does the <u>a</u> make?

Can you see why the <u>a</u> in c<u>a</u>ke makes
a different sound from the <u>a</u> in b<u>a</u>g?

2

EXERCISE 1

Find the right word.

1 My mother cut the (came, cake, case).
2 Hurry up or you will be (late, lake,
   gate).
3 Please close the (gave, game, gate).
4 The doctor (case, came, cake) because
   I was ill.

5 The water in the (take, make, lake)
   was still.
6 I open my book at (shape, page, game)
   one.
7 When we meet we (shape, same,
   shake) hands.
8 Ted (take, ate, face) too many sweets.
9 (Wave, Save, Gave) your flag when the
   Queen passes.
10 My sister (gave, wave, save) me a
   slice of (came, cake, make).

comprehension. Both series are by A. E. Tansley and are published by Arnold.

The *Griffin readers*

Ten- to twelve-year-old slow learners of more normal social and emotional maturity often do well with the *Griffin readers*. These, also published by Arnold, are written by Sheila McCullough. The author has a rare gift of arousing dramatic mood and imagery with quite simple language. The problem of identification is tackled well by basing the series on fantasy, in this case the adventures of three pirates, with a most gripping and powerful story line. There is excellent repetition, especially in the first three books in the scheme. The early books are very thin and contain few words. The success achieved by this easy start gives the youngsters the confidence to tackle the later books in the scheme. By book four they are well into the story and the sheer interest of the content is usually enough to motivate the majority into finishing the scheme. A word of warning about book five, *The storm*. I, in company with many other teachers using this scheme, have found this book a major challenge. After a comparatively simple book four *The storm* bristles with readability difficulties, in fact many teachers rate book six as much easier. Difficult vocabulary and concepts plus quite complex sentence structures interrupt the previous comparatively gentle learning gradient with a jolt. Be prepared, therefore, to put in some hard work at this stage. Prepare this book thoroughly so that you can anticipate and isolate the difficulties your pupil is likely to meet. Teach new concepts and vocabulary before they come up in the text. Take the book slowly, a little at a time. If your pupil gets through this book successfully he should have little difficulty in completing the series. The *Griffin readers* are supported by a set of excellent workbooks, which reinforce by writing,

Ben turned back to the wheel, and looked to see that the ship was on the right course. But as he looked ahead, he saw something black on the sea, far away.

21

drawing, puzzles and games the vocabulary and concepts developed in the reading scheme. I would regard the use of these workbooks as essential, bearing in mind that slow learners need much greater practice and reinforcement at every stage than children of average or above average ability.

The Ward Lock *Secondary remedial workshop*

Slow learners over twelve, provided they have some independence, can put pen to paper and can work on their own for up to thirty minutes at a time, should derive great benefit from working with the *Secondary remedial workshop* published by Ward Lock Educational. The content is very well geared to the needs and interests of adolescents and includes such topics as meeting friends in the coffee bar, going to the youth club and baby-sitting. The readability levels are extremely simple. The designers have looked at a range of reading skills which adolescents would need to use in their daily lives and have built the content around the progressive development of those skills. It is one of the few resource packs available which sets out to teach the use of context and to develop comprehension beyond merely literal levels.

Stott's programmed reading kit
Finally, remember that every learning step achieved by a typical slow learner is only made after exceptional effort by the child. Where the average child takes new learning in his stride the slow learner has to slog at it every inch of the way. Wherever possible, therefore, try to take the 'slog' out of the learning situation by introducing an element of fun. Very gifted teachers can make each learning step into a light-hearted game or enjoyable activity. Help in this direction can be given if you are familiar with the manual to *Stott's programmed reading kit*, published by Holmes McDougall. The manual gives detailed guidance to the use of all the items in the kit, many of which can be used to support your own particular approach. The *Touch cards* are an admirable and effective way of teaching the letter sounds and symbols while the *Half moons* simplify the task of blending the letters into syllables and words. I would regard these two items of equipment and the accompanying manual as quite indispensable to the teacher of slow learning children. Where the manual is particularly useful is that you can adapt many of the ideas in it to the teaching and reinforcement of many of the words in your own reading scheme. Flash cards can be a dull way of achieving recognition through repetition. Instead of putting them on flash cards hard words in your reading scheme can form the material for the *Portholes* game which most slow learners enjoy. Similarly many of the phonic

combinations can be practised in the *Brick wall*, while the longer vowel sounds can be learned most enjoyably with the *Snakes game*. None of the games in this kit are infantile, in fact I personally know of many adult illiterates who found the activities both useful and enjoyable.

Underachieving readers

I use the term 'underachieving readers' to differentiate them from slow learners. In the case of the latter, backwardness is due mainly to intellectual immaturity whereas underachieving readers can often approach average, or even be well above average, intelligence. The potential is there but it has not been realised. The causes of reading underachievement could stem from social inexperience or emotional handicaps such as shyness or timidity. Motivation is an important factor and in many children the desire to learn to read is completely lacking. Physical defects such as poor sight, hearing and articulation are not the handicaps they once were thanks to improved medical services, but it is important to refer children to the appropriate specialist services where you do have any doubts. Many children develop negative attitudes towards reading by being put on books too soon and experiencing failure right at the start. However, in my experience, the commonest cause of reading retardation is frequent or prolonged absence from school at critical stages in the learning process.

Assessment of the problem

As with the slow learner it is necessary to ascertain as precisely as possible the nature of the problem. The more measures we can apply the more accurate will be the resulting profile. Measures of reading age, IQ and relevant reading records should be drawn on wherever possible. It is most important to ascertain that the child is not a slow learner but has the potential to learn at a fair pace given effective treatment. How effective the treatment will be will depend on your ability to interpret the results of testing for these will indicate the type of programme needed.

Word recognition tests

In the first place you should set a Word recognition test, e.g. the *Burt test*, published by Hodder and Stoughton. Get the child to read as many words as he can, stopping him when he has made ten consecutive errors. Calculate his reading age by totalling the words read (i.e. pronounced and accented) correctly. Calculate reading age as follows:

$$\text{reading age} = \frac{\text{number of words read correctly}}{10} + 5,$$

e.g. Michael reads 31 words correctly hence his

$$\text{reading age} = \frac{31}{10} + 5 = 8 \cdot 1.$$

This measure will give you a good idea of the degree of retardation; e.g. if Michael is 12 years old he is about 4 years behind in reading. The two measures used here, reading age and chronological age, should both be taken into account when selecting material for Michael to read: e.g. interest level should be suitable for twelve-year-olds but it should be written at the reading level of a child just eight years old, or preferably somewhat below if he is not going to be kept constantly at full stretch.

Sentence reading tests

Secondly, set a sentence reading test, such as the *Holborn reading scale*, published by Harrap. This, too, will give you a reading age but it will probably be lower than that obtained on the *Burt test*. This is because the *Holborn test*

has a ceiling (jargon for highest possible score) one year lower than the *Burt test*. Get the child to read the sentences and stop him when he has made four errors. At the end of each line of print there is a four-digit number. This is the reading age disguised; e.g. the number at the end of the line in which your reader's fourth mistake occurs is 1009. The first two digits refer to years and the last two to months, hence on this test your child has a reading age of 10 years 9 months. Similarly the number 0911 indicates a reading age of 9 years 11 months. Such a device obviates the need for calculation.

Diagnostic use of reading tests

The two tests mentioned will not only give you a score. They will also give you valuable opportunities to observe and assess your reader's strengths and weaknesses. The *Burt test* consists of isolated words where sequential or contextual clues do not operate. Consequently the child has to recognise the words instantly (and he can do this if they have been consolidated into his sight vocabulary) or he has to work them out with whatever attack skills he has acquired. He has to work out unfamiliar words by phonic analysis and recognise irregularities when they occur. The first thirty words test a knowledge of the short vowel sounds and the most frequently used single consonants. Thereafter longer vowels and double consonants proliferate and words become progressively polysyllabic. Thus it is possible to use this test diagnostically if you familiarise yourself with its phonic and syllabification progressions.

The *Holborn reading scale* encourages reading in context and thus gives opportunities for you to observe and note many common faults such as wild guessing, omission, substitution, eye wandering, word-by-word reading, inadequate focussing, disregard of punctuation and ineptitude in phonic analysis. The two tests

to   is   up   he   at

for   my   sun   one   of

big   some   his   or   an

went   boys   that   girl   water

just   day   wet   pot   things

no   told   love   now   sad

nurse   carry   quickly   village   scramble

---

motionless   ultimate   atmosphere   reputation   binocular

economy   theory   humanity   philosopher   contemptuous

autobiography   excessively   champagne   terminology   perambulating

efficiency   unique   perpetual   mercenary   glycerine

influential   atrocious   fatigue   exorbitant   physician

microscopical   contagion   renown   hypocritical   fallacious

phlegmatic   melancholy   palpable   eccentricity   constitutionally

alienate   phthisis   poignancy   ingratiating   subtlety

THE BURT WORD READING TEST (1974 REVISION)

NAME_____   SCORE_____

SCHOOL _____   READING AGE_____

DATE OF TEST _____AGE_____   MENTAL AGE_____
(IF KNOWN)

DATE OF BIRTH_____   EXAMINER'S INITIALS_____

HOLBORN READING SCALE

1. The dog got wet and Tom had to rub him dry. — 509

2. He was a very good boy to give you some of his sweets. — 600

3. My sister likes me to open my book and read to her. — 603

4. Go away and hide behind that door where we found you just now. — 606

5. Please don't let anyone spoil these nice fresh flowers. — 609

6. The string had eight knots in it which I had to untie. — 700

7. Wine is made from the juice of grapes which grow in warm countries. — 703

8. Mary went to the grocer's and bought some sugar and some syrup. — 706

9. Quench your thirst by drinking a glass of our sparkling ginger ale. — 709

10. The people could scarcely obtain enough food to remain healthy. — 800

11. Elizabeth had her hair thoroughly combed and her fringe cut. — 803

12. By stretching up, George just managed to touch the garage ceiling. — 806

13. Father had a brief telephone conversation with my cousin Philip. — 809

14. This coupon entitled you to a specimen piece of our delicious toffee. — 900

15. The chemist could not suggest a satisfactory remedy for my headache. — 903

16. Nobody recognised Roger in his disguise as a police official. — 906

17. Leonard was engaged by the Irish Linen Association to act as their London agent. — 909

described enable you to highlight specific disabilities. Once you know what these are you can then set about treating them.

Testing phonic skill

Many retarded readers lack skill in phonic analysis. This may result from frequent or prolonged absence from school at early stages in the reading process or from over-emphasis on look and say methods in many infant schools. Whatever the reason, if such weakness exists it will be highlighted by the diagnostic use of the *Burt* and *Holborn tests*. It then becomes necessary to ascertain precisely which phonic combinations are causing the trouble. You will be greatly helped in ascertaining these by setting the *Swansea test of phonic skills*, published by Basil Blackwell. In the past many children have been falsely diagnosed as having considerable

Name _____ Sex _____

Age (years and completed months) _____ years _____ months

1

> wok
> lok
> mok
> rok
> pok

2

> ced
> ved
> jed
> yed
> hed

Pages	1	2	3,4,5	6	7	Total
Max.	(S.V.) 10	(L.V.) 10	(I.L.B.) 24	(F.L.B.) 12	(MIS) 9	65
Score						

Examiner's Comments:

(i) Special weakness(es)

(ii) Other comments

(iii) Recommendations

Examiner _____

Date _____

phonic skill because they can pronounce and spell accurately words which conform to accepted phonic conventions. Actually it is possible to learn such words by sight methods without knowing the letter sounds involved. The *Swansea test* assesses phonic skill by getting the children to identify and reconstruct the phonic conventions by means of unfamiliar nonsense syllables. There is an excellent manual with clear directions for administering the test and for scoring and analysis. Once the specific weaknesses have been identified by the use of this test the reader can then be set to work at the appropriate exercises in *Sound sense* supported possibly by a suitable game or activity from *Stott's programmed reading kit*. Incidentally, unlike the *Burt* and *Holborn tests* which have to be set individually, the *Swansea test* is a group test and can be set to quite a sizeable group of children.

The illustrated sentence below is from K. Goodman 'Miscues: windows on the reading process' in Miscues Analysis *edited by Goodman, ERIC Clearinghouse on Reading and Communication Skills, NCTE, USA*

There are two newer and more informal methods of testing and diagnosing reading difficulties – miscue analaysis and one involving close procedure. We asked Dr. Elizabeth Goodacre to describe and illustrate the two methods which will also be included in the radio series that accompany this book.

Miscue analysis

Reading miscue analysis was begun in 1963 by Kenneth Goodman in the United States for the express purpose of providing knowledge of the reading process and how it is used and acquired. It is his belief that this knowledge in turn, can form the basis for more effective teaching reading techniques. Goodman, and his colleagues believe that nothing the reader does when reading, is accidental. Mistakes or as he prefers to call them *miscues*, when the reader reads something different from what appears in the text, are the reader's attempt to process the print to get at meaning. Goodman suggested that if we can understand how the reader's miscues relate to what is expected to be read, we can begin to understand how the child is using the reading process.

Here is a sentence from a story used in Goodman's research, and the miscues the pupil made when reading it. (You will find a code that I use for reading miscues on p. 38.)

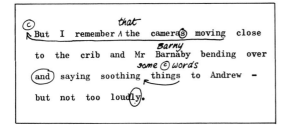

In this sentence the reader leaves out a word and some parts of words, substitutes other words, goes back at times to correct himself,

and ends up with a meaningful sentence. Goodman suggests that we should be concerned with more than his superficial behaviour. We must infer from it the process he used and his competence with that process. He put the word *that* but corrected when he realised the pattern he had made was not acceptable grammatically. He left out *and* but did not correct this because it was not necessary – it made sense. In miscue analysis, you start with observed behaviour, but you do not stop there. You can, through analysis of the miscues, see the process at work. In this form of informal assessment, you have a window on the reading process.

What does the reader do, when he begins to experience difficulty? Usually he asks himself what would make sense, what would fit the grammatical structure (the rules of language usage), and generally then, only what would match the graphic clues – the look of the word and still fit into the meaning and structure of the sentence as a whole. This keeps the value of the graphic information in proper perspective and does not cause the reader to use any more information than is absolutely necessary.

Readers who are inefficient are often too much concerned with word-for-word accuracy which may show up as:
● Supplying a word which matches closely on a visual basis but not as regards meaning.
● Frequent correction of miscues which do not really affect the meaning.
● Several attempts at getting the pronunciation of a word right, even when it makes little difference to the understanding of a passage; e.g. struggling with unfamiliar character names, place names, foreign words, etc.

To assess the proficiency of a reader Goodman has suggested that it might be better to use a procedure such as the following:

1 Count the reader's miscues.

2 Subtract all those which are shifts to the reader's own dialect (reading *we was going* for *we were going*) because these are not really mistakes but rather probably the way the reader 'talks to himself' or how he thinks;
3 Count all miscues resulting in acceptable meaning.
4 Count all miscues which result in unacceptable meaning but which the reader successfully corrects.
5 Add the miscues in steps 3 and 4. The result is the total number of miscues semantically acceptable or corrected.

This last score, expressed as a percentage of all miscues, is what Goodman has come to call the *comprehending score* of the reader. He sees it as a measure of the reader's ability to keep his sights firmly on the meaning. It is a measure of the quality of the reader's miscues. What is important is not *how many* mistakes are made but how they effect the meaning.

Although many teachers in this country find the idea of using pupils' reading mistakes constructively an attractive idea, there is a certain feeling that Goodman's approach may be too radical and will lead to sloppy, careless and inaccurate reading, that such an approach will interfere with the child's developing grasp of the code aspect of reading (the correspondence between letter strings and their sounds) and mastery of word attack skills.
Most teachers, however, are involved in assessing children's reading; one way or another. Perhaps we should remember that when we judge the progress of very young children learning to speak, you do this quite simply. If they can make themselves understood, they are learning to talk; if they can reply when spoken to, they are learning to listen. In other words, you judge their success on the basis of the progress they make in using language for

particular purposes. Reading also needs to be judged in this way. To what extent are children in your classes learning from an increasing range of written language – reading and understanding different styles of written work (descriptive, expositional, analytical, etc), verse and dramatic forms, reports and instructions, the characteristic language forms of the different content areas, magazines and newspapers, and official forms and documentary evidence. Goodman suggests:
'We let ourselves confuse published reading tests with the competence in reading they are trying to assess. The subskill tests, skill check lists, and word lists do not test ability to understand written language. They test, in large part, ability to perform with the abstract bits and pieces of language.'

Miscue analysis and hearing children read
Miscue analyses follow a relatively uniform procedure. A story, usually a complete one, is used which is sufficiently difficult for the pupil to make somewhere between twenty-five and fifty miscues – sufficient for any pattern of miscues to emerge. The teacher has a copy of the material to be read. The pupil is encouraged to use any strategies he knows to read unknown words, to guess or to skip a word, but the teacher does not help other than by general words of encouragement. After the story has been read, the pupil is asked to tell it in his own words. After the uninterrupted re-telling, the pupil is asked open-ended questions about any aspects of the story that have been omitted. A comprehension rating is made on an analysis of the re-telling and the miscues are coded according to a particular analytic procedure developed by Yetta Goodman. The whole procedure, reading and re-telling is taped.
   This is a somewhat complicated procedure

Code for recording miscues		
Sentence to be read	**She was washing up in the kitchen**	
Error type	*Coding*	*Example*
Substitution	Underline and write in the word substituted	*were* She was washing up in the kitchen
Non-response	Dotted line under the word if reader waits to be prompted or asks	She was washing up in the <u>kitchen</u>
Insertion	Add additional word/s or part-word added	*out* She was washing up in the kitchen
Omission	Circle word/s left out	She was washing (up) in the kitchen
Pause	Stroke, use when reader pauses for more than two seconds	She was washing/up in the kitchen
Repetition	Mark the word/s repeated with a curved line	*R* She was washing up in the kitchen
Correction*	Write in original miscue, then curved line with the letter (c) for self-correction	(c) *had been* (c) *bowl* She was washing up in the kitchen

*Clay (1969) found in her study of beginners that her 'high' progress group not only made fewer mistakes than the 'low' group but also differed in their correction of errors. The 'high' group corrected one in three or four errors in comparison with the 'low' group's error correction rate of one in twenty.

which is perhaps more suitable for in-depth work with teachers or for research purposes. But some of the basic principles can be used in the more familiar classroom hearing situation. The following ways of recording and analysing children's miscues have been used by teachers:

● The teacher can use duplicated copies of particular pages from graded reading books, recording the child's miscues on the copy and filing it as a record of progress.

● A sheet of acetate can be placed over the page in the teacher's copy of the book being read, and miscues recorded on this while the child reads from his book. The acetate can be wiped clean and reused after observations are noted in the teacher's record book.

● A cassette tape recorder can be used, recording the pupil's errors during the playback. As the teacher is not involved in recording errors during hearing, she has more chance to observe other aspects of the situation; e.g. pupil's attitude, signs of fatigue, etc.

Even if this more detailed type of hearing cannot be regularly carried out, teachers have suggested that this more systematic approach and the subsequent insights into the reading process, continue to have beneficial effects on their hearing of their pupils. They find themselves asking questions such as 'Why did he read that? Is the meaning still acceptable even though he has made a mistake? It doesn't make sense, is he going to correct himself? If he substitutes a word, is his word the same part of speech? How close is his word to the sound and shape of the word he should have read? Why did he read *that*?'

Code for recording miscues

On the next page is a record made after hearing one pupil, Paul, read in this way Paul is thirteen years ten months and is reading a passage (complete in itself) which has been written at a level of difficulty of RA 8 (Fry Readability formula).

HALLOWE'EN NIGHT

Just before midnight on Hallowe'en, Alison was lying in *the* ~~or/see - Ep~~ Alison. *leaving/laying*

bed. Suddenly / there was a tinkling of glass and a gush *tapping* *crashing of/crash*

of wind. Alison sat up and looked around. There sitting *R*

on the floor was a witch! She was disentangling herself *dancing/decide* *R*

from her broomstick. *for she*

"Oh," said Alison, "what are you doing here?"

"That's a good question," said the witch. "I must have
taken a wrong turning at the last set of chimney pots. *Turn* *kitchen spoons*
I shall be late." *long ©* *(* sound of dishing up from kitchens)*

"Can I help?" asked Alison.
They tried this
"The trouble / is my broomstick / is broken and I've left *I/broom* *R*
my spell book / at home. You see I haven't been a witch *R back*
for very long and I can't remember many spells. Do you *can/©* *my* *Don't*
know any spells for / mending broomsticks?" *a mēd*

"Not really," said Alison, "but we have a broomstick

downstairs. Would that help?"
a
"Yes, I remember the spell to make / broomsticks fly."
kept © *before*
Alison crept downstairs and brought back the broomstick.
remember
"Oh you are good," said the witch. "I will return the

broomstick. Goodbye." *anythink / any words* *fun ©*

Before Alison could say another word the witch had flown

away into the night.

Paul tries to anticipate meaning on the basis of his knowledge of language. In the very first line, he read Hallowe'en as if it was the name of something, the subject of an action, which then has to be fitted on to Alison – the teacher helps him with this name and he can then get 'laying in bed'. He probably is clueing from the beginning letters of words (e.g. tinkling/tapping; disentangling/dancing; late/long; trouble/tried; broken/broom; etc.). Sometimes he is able to self correct (see four instances). What helped him to realise a word didn't make sense? Why were other miscues not corrected? Did they sound like language – make sense to him? What about 'kitchen spoons'? Was this a substitution just to keep going, prompted by the noises in the room next door. Goodman has a collection of miscues from many parts of the world and apparently food (kitchen?) substitutions are particularly common, especially before dinner!

Paul is not too happy with the switch from the specific, individual 'broomstick' to the use of 'broomsticks' as a class or group name. Each line he inserts 'a' before 'broomsticks' and omits the plural 's'. I think he has difficulty with the word 'mending' because he is anticipating it as a word describing the 'broomstick' rather than the verb 'mending'. This may be important as he has not read 'broom' and so has not really understood that the writer intends the reader to think that the witch has broken her broomstick crashing through the window. It is worth looking at the text and seeing just how explicit is this idea. Having tried this text with a number of children, I know that some of them do not think she crashed through the window, and are uncertain why she needs to borrow Alison's broomstick.

Finally, here is Paul's account of what the story was about. How does his retelling relate to his reading of the text? What is omitted? What has he remembered – do any phrases come directly from the text? What has he put into his own words and therefore inferred? The story is supposed to be suitable for RA 8, but can be a measure based on length of word and length of sentence, measure effectively the imagery involved in the text? The clarity of the writer's intentions to communicate with the reader are very important at any age.

'About a witch landing in Alison's house and she used the wrong spell . . . because she wanted to go . . . and her . . . she couldn't . . . to remember the spell . . . and when she gave her another broom from downstairs she remembered the spell.'

T: 'And what did she do then?'
Paul: 'And then she went.'

Cloze procedure

The teacher can use cloze to find out more about a particular pupil's understanding of a passage or book. Words are deleted on a regular basis (e.g. every fifth or tenth word) and pupils are asked to fill in the spaces or gaps (usually indicated by a line of regular length). The pupil's task is to read the passage silently and write in the missing word on the blank line. Cloze procedure 'purists' argue that only exact replacement of the deleted words should be counted correct and that a correct score of about 40 per cent indicates that a pupil understands the material. This criterion is based on statistical analyses which separate good and poor readers as correlated with scores on other reading tests.

Errors, words which are not exact replacements of the deleted words, can be analysed to see if they are semantically and/or syntactically appropriate. Smith and Johnson (1976) suggest that a pupil 'who misses all the words in terms of exact replacement but whose responses

THE MONKEYS

One day, a circus was going along the road from one town

to another. Most people were fast asleep in _bed_ ✓ [bed],

but the circus people had been up _on_ very early, and

now, as they went on _There_ ✓ [their] way, they passed green

fields and dark _comes_ woods [woods] and slow running rivers.

✓ Then the monkey [waggon] cart _had_ lost a wheel and went right

over _to_ on its side. The roof fell off and _the_ ✓

monkeys climbed out. Twenty of them !

✓

Over _the_ ✓ fields they ran and into the woods.

they ✓ went swinging in the trees, and some went

climing ✓ over fences and running into a farmyard, ringing

the bell and peeping through windows.

---

constitute reasonable synonyms probably has no reading problem, in our judgment, or at least has a different kind of problem from a child whose answers are semantically bizarre or ambiguous or who leave a half page of blank lines. They recommend cloze as a way of diagnosing the pupil's semantic-syntactic contextual 'sense'.

The example above was completed by Paul, whose miscue we examined before. The passage is approximately RA 9–10 (Fry) and Paul gets a correct score of 60 per cent. It should be remembered that Paul is nearly fourteen. All four errors are syntactic and suggest that Paul uses anticipation in his reading but cannot always check his predictions by accurately processing the material which comes after the gap. In discussing his answers, when the teacher was 'reading over' the gap for him, he was able to suggest 'woods' and 'waggon' – appropriate answers for noun slots in the text. This tendency (to anticipate meaning mainly on the basis of what has just been read) was also shown in his miscue. Clay (1972) has suggested that the competent reader needs to develop 'a smooth predict and check' procedure. Paul is predicting but his checking strategies seem at fault.

Readability factors

As well as treating specific weaknesses as they are identified it is also necessary to promote fluency, concentration and the ability to read at some length. For infants at the beginning stage most infant reading schemes aim to develop these abilities by providing supplementary readers at every level. Where there is no comparable provision for the adolescent backward reader, for whom there are no comprehensive reading schemes as such, you have to look around for materials which will do the job satisfactorily. This is complicated by the following constraints. The content needs to be comparatively adult while the presentation needs to be simple: e.g. at the lowest levels backward readers need big bold print well spaced for ease of discrimination, with few words to a line to promote effective eye movements, with a simple vocabulary load and concept level, with the whole arranged in short, simple sentence structures.

The *Wide range readers*

With care, you could select some of the material in the *Wide range readers*, published by Oliver and Boyd, to suit your pupil and still observe the readability constraints specified above. There are twelve books in this series, with two books, one blue, one green at each level. The blue and green books within each level are parallel in difficulty. They are graded for readability as follows:

Books 1, blue and green   Reading age   7·0– 7·5
Books 2, blue and green   Reading age   7·5– 8·0
Books 3, blue and green   Reading age   8·0– 8·5
Books 4, blue and green   Reading age   8·5– 9·0
Books 5, blue and green   Reading age   9·0–10·0
Books 6, blue and green   Reading age   10·0–11·0

At the lowest levels some of the material is naturally juvenile and you would need to select those stories which would satisfy the needs of your particular reader. In addition to the books mentioned above, there are the *Wide range interest readers*, one at each of the readability levels of the standard readers referred to above. These have a largely factual, non-infantile content and would more nearly satisfy the needs of your older backward readers. They include simple questions testing literal comprehension and focus the reader's attention on the recall or recognition of the main facts and supporting details in each text.

Functional readability levels

Once you get away from the tight structure of schemes like *Wide range* and draw on books from the wider range of literature beyond you will help your pupil by being aware of the different readability levels within which you will both have to function.

Instructional level

When you are working one to one with your pupil, teaching him some new skill or giving him practice in perfecting it, you will be working at his instructional level. This means that on such occasions he will be at full stretch, e.g. he has a reading age of 8·0, therefore in order to get him to forge ahead and make progress you will be teaching him at levels slightly above his capacity. This is why short bursts of teaching activity are recommended, followed by time for practice and reinforcement, otherwise your pupil would not be able to stand the pace and would find the learning task beyond him if work were always at such a level.

Independent level

This is the level when your pupil is reading for enjoyment either books which you have prescribed because you think he will like them or which he has chosen himself. This is the role of the 'supplementary' reading matter referred to above. Such material helps him to develop fluency, to extend his own interests and to increase his concentration and speed of silent reading. He should be able to cope with it without outside help. I would suggest that independent reading level is at least one year below the child's reading age. Thus if you were to use the *Wide range* series as supplementary readers you would be wise to ensure that your pupil has a reading age above 8·0 before putting him on Book 1.

Frustration level

This is the level when the material is so difficult that the reader gives up trying. Obviously you should try to avoid getting your pupils in this state, but frequently this is easier said than done. In order to guarantee that the material you select or recommend is below frustration level and for general reading for information and pleasure is actually at your pupils' independent level you have to take into account the following factors:

1 the reader's interests,
2 his reading age,
3 the readability level of the text.

It is comparatively easy to ascertain factors 1 and 2. Factor 3 is the hard one. Imagine you have a backward reader with reading age 9·0 who is keen on aircraft. There are many books on aircraft but you cannot tell merely by looking at them which one has the right readability level, say about reading age 8·0, for this particular pupil. In such a case, use the 5 per cent rule, thus: give your pupil a book which you think is right for him; get him to read aloud to you a page or two at random; make a note of all the errors he makes; if the errors constitute more than 5 per cent (one error on average every twenty words) the book is too hard. Try again with different books on the same topic until you get one with the average error rate below 5 per

cent. (See also pages 87 and 101 for more information on readability.)

Organising reading with slow learners and underachieving readers

The junior/middle school

There is no doubt in my mind that, of the ten- to sixteen-year-olds experiencing difficulty in reading, the ones most likely to get effective help are those aged ten and eleven. Such children will still be in junior school. It is here that conditions for teaching reading are most favourable. The children are with their own teacher for most of each school day. If the class teacher accepts the challenge of working with slow learning or retarded readers it is possible to time-table specific periods of instruction as well as to give incidental help at other times in the day. The teacher has time to observe the child in many different situations, to get to know his strengths and weaknesses, his needs and interests. All this knowledge can be brought to bear in drawing up a suitable programme.

Some schools have floating teachers who withdraw children in need of help with reading for either individual or group instruction. This can be most valuable especially when it is additional or supplementary to the on-going help provided by the class teacher. To be effective, however, there needs to be constant liaison between 'floater' and class teacher. The latter needs to follow up work initiated in the withdrawal period. All too often when there is a withdrawal system (and this applies also to the poorer kinds of peripatetic remedial service) the only result is to absolve class teachers from taking a hand in remedial work. They do not regard it as their concern. Not only do they thus lose valuable opportunities for professional growth but they leave certain children floundering for most of each school day, a constant prey to boredom or disruptiveness.

Many LEAs are now reorganising their former remedial service into an advisory service. The erstwhile remedial teachers are now advisory teachers. Instead of withdrawing children for specialist help they now go into classrooms working alongside the class teachers and helping them with methods and materials. I am sure that this is a step in the right direction. An even more desirable innovation would be the early implementation of one of the major recommendations of the Bullock report that there should be a language specialist in every school. The spare capacity in the teacher-training industry makes the present time most opportune for the training of such badly needed personnel.

In some junior schools children with severe reading problems are withdrawn into full-time remedial classes. If the provision is good, i.e. with trained staff and an adequate range of teaching materials, such help can be effective. Often, however, such conditions do not prevail and the children fail to acquire motivation and a sense of standards. When this kind of organisation is not working the children are better returned to their ordinary classes. It is then up to the head of the school to initiate a 'reading drive' and to help each class teacher to teach her own 'problem' children to read.

A recent innovation is the possibility of counselling approaches for those who, in addition to reading failure, show signs of emotional disturbance. The theory behind these approaches is that it is possible to accelerate the remedial reading process by systematically taking steps to improve the child's self-image. If you are the head of a junior school, you might like to investigate these ideas further. You will find them in *Improved reading through counselling* written by Denis Lawrence and published by Ward Lock Educational. If you are a secondary head, don't be put off looking at these methods by Lawrence's warning that as yet, without further research, they must be considered as suitable for juniors only.

The secondary school

The organisational problems peculiar to our secondary schools make it very difficult for effective help in reading to be given to slow learners and underachieving readers. Narrow subject specialisation and the rigid time-tabling associated with it often result in no one knowing the children well enough or having sufficient time to help backward readers. Indeed, until very recently, few secondary teachers considered the teaching of reading to be any concern of theirs.

The varied curriculum of the secondary school makes demands on reading skill far in excess of those considered necessary in primary school. Different subjects demand different reading strategies, great speed of recognition is necessary, study becomes an increasingly important factor, and accessing and locating skills, as well as the ability to summarise information and apply it, must be acquired if the pupil is to make headway. Secondary schools have been generally slow to acknowledge that many children gain little benefit from specialist teaching because they cannot cope with the reading involved. There are three possible solutions to this problem and only one is commonly adopted in schools. This is the establishment of remedial departments which withdraw the children for periodic instruction or organise them into full-time remedial classes. Given optimum conditions, particularly staff specifically trained and qualified in remedial work, some excellent work is being done. One fact, however, has not been sufficiently recognised, namely that such special teaching is only effective if it is maintained. The goal of the teaching is to work up the children to

45

the average standard for their age and then return them to their normal classes. Few children who have had long periods of withdrawal for remedial purposes can cope confidently with the transition to normal standards. Therefore the special treatment should persist until long after the apparent need for it has passed.

A second possibility involves a challenge to which few secondary teachers have yet responded. This is to put the onus for teaching the reading of each specialist subject on the specialist teacher of each subject. No one knows better than he the vocabulary and concepts involved and the stages and progressions by which those concepts are acquired. If (cf. Bullock) each school had a reading specialist to give advice and support in planning a reading programme to the other subject specialists the paths to learning could be eased for many children who are at present in difficulty.

If early specialisation (with all the possible reading demands which this entails) is a major stumbling block to backward readers, why not defer it for a year or two? The first year in secondary school could more usefully be regarded as a year in which reading skill could be consolidated and weaknesses put right. Surely what is needed is for each school to draw up an inventory or checklist of all the reading skills that the children will need to meet successfully the demands of the different specialisms and to spend the first two years ensuring that they acquire them. They could then really forge ahead in subsequent years.

The non–reader

There may be in your school some children between ten and sixteen years of age who, for all practical purposes, cannot read at all. They may know just a few isolated words. It is likely that these same children cannot write even the simplest connected sentence. Writing for them is merely copying. Now, if you have some determination, you could find that such children are often easier to teach than those who have already made a start. One of the major problems in teaching remedial pupils lies in unravelling what they know from what they don't know. Many of the problems of the remedial pupil are more in the fields of spelling or writing than in reading. However, when the children have learned nothing at all there is only one place to start – at the very beginning.

Some basic principles

● When a pupil has reached adolescence and can hardly read a single word you have to concede that all the approaches that have been tried have failed. If they have not worked in the past there is little likelihood that they will work in the future. Therefore your only chance of teaching such a pupil to read lies in using a new approach, one that has no associations with previous failure.

● When a child has failed for so long he must be rewarded. The only way you can do this is by giving him success.

● Time is crucial to the older non-reader. The child starting in infant school expects that over two or three years he will gradually grow into reading and writing. Older failures have been through this stage and have not succeeded. For those nearing the end of the period of schooling there is not the time for gradual success. A dynamic approach is needed which gives instant success and the success must be maintained.

● In order to carry out the above principles you must eschew halfheartedness. Your pupil, you must remember, has possibly had many half-hearted people attempting to teach him. They have not helped him in the past, no matter how well-meaning they have been, and so he regards them as failures too. He will not co-operate in half-hearted approaches. Hence you must have confidence in your ability. Show him you mean business and can deliver the goods.

● Traditional remedial methods have failed the older non-reader because they work on the pupil's weaknesses. You will only succeed if you work on his strengths.

● It follows that if you work from your pupil's strengths you will use methods which are uniquely personal to that pupil. They are *his* strengths and no one else's. Hence your methods will be personalised rather than individualised. So-called individualisation in the teaching of reading often involves a one-to-one teacher–pupil relationship. On investigation, though the child is taken on his own, it is only done in order to fit him to a mass approach – the typical reading scheme which was designed not specifically to teach your particular non-reader but for thousands of other children. Personalised approaches involve the application of sound teaching methods to the unique strengths of the non-reader.

A language experience approach

You may wonder, when a child has got to secondary school still not reading, what strengths you could possibly draw on in order to teach him. Yet, on examination, many adolescent non-readers seem in every way perfectly normal except that they can neither read nor write. If they can speak, see and hear, you can teach them to read. These are their strengths. It may be that, compared with some other children, their speech is limited both in quality and quantity. But it is the only language they know and you must use what is there in order to make a start.

Reading starts with perception. The printed symbols cause a mental reaction and the mind attempts to interpret the meaning of the symbols. The first stage in this interpretative process is recognition (re-knowing). At the early stages of learning to read you can only recognise (know again) words you know already. These have to be acquired first in speech before you can recognise, then understand, them in print.

To begin with, make a deal with your pupil. Tell him you are going to take him each day at a certain time for, say, twenty minutes. If by the end of the week he is still not reading tell him that the teaching will stop.

Day 1

The next stage is to get him to talk. Four or five sentences is enough to start with. The usual problem here is that the child will not speak in sentences. Therefore, taking care not to put words in his mouth (because it is *his* words that are wanted, not yours), pattern his responses so that sentences result. Suppose for example you want information about the following:

his name   his age   his address   his hobby

You may start thus and ask:
'What's your name?'
His reply may well be:
'Billy.'
Now the response you want is:
'My name is Billy.'
Show him what you want (i.e. pattern the desired response) by saying:
'O.K. Now you ask me my name.'
He asks:
'What's your name?'
You reply (e.g.):
'My name is Mr Walker. Let's try again. What's your name?'
His reply:
'My name is Billy Robinson.'
Let us say that by means of such patterning you get from him four sentences in the following order:

My name is Billy Robinson.
I am fourteen years old.
I live at 25 The Ringway.
My hobby is watching United.

Write it down, in the exact order in which he says it, on a pad (you may need to do this quickly). Then say, 'Is that what you just said?'

He will agree (he only said it seconds before). Tell him that if he can say that and remember it, then he can read it. Read it to him once again and get him to repeat it. He will do this with minimal help from you because he remembers the words just uttered and repeated, and, more important, the order in which he said them.

Now show him the words *in writing*. Have ready two large cards, each ruled with faint pencilled lines about an inch apart and wide enough to take each of the short sentences to a line. Print them *in pencil* in big, bold print, well spaced, like the example on the next page.

As you finish each word say it aloud and make your pupil repeat it after you. At each full stop say aloud the whole sentence you have just written and make him repeat that after you.

Give the pupil a black felt pen and make him trace over the four pencilled sentences you have just made. As he writes (i.e. traces) each word say it aloud and make him repeat it. Do the same with each sentence. By the time your pupil has written the last sentence there will have been many repetitions of the material.

While he is tracing make another copy, with another black felt pen. As you have actually written both, they should be identical. After so many repetitions your pupil will almost certainly be able to read the sentences without difficulty.

Day 2

This day, you should concentrate on teaching the sentences out of sequence, but first revise the previous day's reading and make sure your pupil remembers the material.

Have ready two big envelopes, one with your pupil's name on, the other showing your name. You also need a pair of scissors. Cut your card (not the traced one) into the four sentence strips. Arrange them in random order and ask your pupil to match them to the sentences which he has traced. When he does this with some ease, turn over the master card so that he gets no help from the order of the sentence strips and present them to him in random order. Put in his envelope the sentence strips which he reads correctly. Those where he blunders go in yours. Work on the incorrectly read sentence strips by further matching to the master card and identifying certain distinguishing features. Then bring out the envelopes again and play the sentence game until he knows each sentence perfectly at sight.

Days 3 and 4

Revise the sentences learned the previous day. Then the target for days 3 and 4 is the learning of the separate words at sight, i.e. out of context, in random order.

First arrange the sentence strips in the same order as the sentences on the master card. Take your scissors and the first sentence strip and cut off the words on it in order from left to right. Say each word aloud just before you cut it off and have your pupil repeat it after you. Do this with all the words in the remaining sentences.

Next, taking the words in random order, get your pupil to find them and match them to the words on the master card. When all the words have been matched bring out the two envelopes, remove the master card so that there are no sequential clues and present the words to your pupil in random order. As with the sentence game, use the envelopes to record the words he knows and those he cannot identify. Work on the latter by further matching and repetition until he knows all the words at sight.

My name is Billy Robinson.

I am fourteen years old.

I live at 25 The Ringway.

My hobby is watching United.

Day 5

Use this day to revise the work previously done. Then your pupil can be encouraged to illustrate his work with photographs or his own drawings.

Repeat these procedures each week until your pupil has a sight vocabulary of about 300 words. By then he should be confident enough to begin a non-infantile reading scheme such as *Racing to read* or the *Griffin readers*. He should also by then be able to make progress with some of the activities in *Stott's programmed reading kit*.

For a fuller case history and more detailed discussion of this approach you might refer to my book *Reading development and extension*, chapter 6, published by Ward Lock Educational, 1974.

Teaching the backward reader – some final points

Despite the vogue which 'discovery' methods have enjoyed over the past decade you can be sure that these are useless for children who have severe reading difficulties. If such methods were of any use all children would surely have 'discovered' how to read before the secondary stage of schooling. Teaching is effective – what would Helen Keller have become without her teacher? Special teaching, by specialist trained and qualified personnel, is even more effective, provided that such teaching is maintained. Remember, too, that intelligence and social background are not decisive factors. All but the most severely handicapped children can read if well taught.

Summary

In this chapter I have categorised failing readers into underachievers and slow learners. I have suggested how, by testing and observation, such classifications can be made. We must make these distinctions with some accuracy in order to give treatment of the most appropriate kind. I have suggested the use of commercially produced materials for certain teaching purposes. For the most severely retarded I recommend most strongly the language experience approach. Here we draw on the child's own language and experience to make his own personal 'reading scheme'.

The slow reader

The *slow reader*, as distinct from slow learner, is one who reads at a slow pace. This can be quite a disability both in school and in adult life, for speed and efficiency are important factors in a modern society. The more common types of slow reading, their causes and methods of remediation are discussed separately below.

Verbalisation

This is one of the most common kinds of slow reading. The reader is unable to read silently and is therefore forced to read aloud, i.e. at the speed of speech. A secondary kind of verbalisation is known as sub-vocalisation. Here the reader mouths the words without saying them aloud. He listens to himself reading with the inner ear. The result is that again he reads only at the speed of speech.

Both these types of slow reading result from over-emphasis on oral reading during the early stages of reading instruction. In such cases the practice of 'hearing children read' has gone on too long and teachers have been unaware of the need to give practice in silent reading. Often this arises because the infant reading scheme adopted has too steep a learning gradient. The children are at frustration level almost all the way through the scheme and have to read aloud to prove both to themselves and to their teacher that they are coping. Alternatively, some teachers short-circuit the learning progressions in the reading scheme and go through it verti-cally; i.e. going through the basic books only and ignoring the horizontal progress that is gained through supplementary reading at each stage.

The remedy for verbalisation is fairly obvious. The children need to be put on very simple material, preferably within their interest range, with a good story line, and to be encouraged by such means to read much more for sheer pleasure. Also teachers need to shift their emphasis from enunciation and pronunciation towards comprehension and content. The more the child can identify with the characters and project himself into the situations the more reading becomes an inward and private process.

Inadequate focussing

Many people read slowly because the eye movements they use in reading are ineffective. We know that when reading the eyes move left to right along each line of print. They then make a backward and downward sweep to the start of the next line. The left-to-right progress along each line is not a smooth continuous movement. It is a series of jerky forward movements and pauses. It is only during the pauses (fixations) that reading occurs. The eyes cannot focus when moving. When the eyes stop and fixate on a section of the print the focus rapidly fans out in all directions so that one part of the print can be seen clearly while on the edges vision is blurred. (See also page 21.) The amount of print that you can see clearly in one fixation is your visual span. Obviously the larger your visual span the more print you can process in each fixation and therefore those with wide spans tend to be faster readers than those with small ones. However, reading is not merely a visual matter. What is seen has to be decoded, so a time factor enters in. Those who take a long time to decode what they see in each fixation tend to be slow readers. To counteract inefficient eye movements in your slow readers you must attempt the following:
● widen the visual span and thereby reduce the frequency of the fixations,
● reduce the duration of the fixations.
It is interesting to note that we can all be slow readers at times. When the material is difficult and unfamiliar we put much more effort into the task than when we read less complex texts. It is, in fact, essential that on such occasions we do

read slowly if the consequences of mis-reading could be damaging. This would depend on how important the reading purpose is to us. However, what is implied here is that the competent reader consciously chooses to be slow in order to accomplish his goal. He can also read fast to satisfy other reading purposes. The slow reader has no such flexibility. He reads all material whether trivial or important at the same slow pace. This is patently inefficient and is analogous to driving a car with a manual gearbox in second gear whatever the driving conditions.

Most of the bad habits observable in the older reader can be traced to instructional weaknesses in the early stages. Poor focussing skills are often due to children being put on reading too soon before their powers of visual discrimination are sufficiently developed for the task. Another visual defect common in the slow reader is eye wandering. The child constantly loses his place and hence the meaning. He has not been taught to make the smooth left-to-right eye movements practised by the competent reader. Frequently children of this type have been kept at near frustration level constantly in their progress through the reading scheme. The opportunity for practice and consolidation of visual skills has been omitted because of insufficient time devoted to supplementary reading at the different stages.

Too early an emphasis on phonic analysis can also retard reading rate. The children look at the letters either separately or in small clusters before blending them into syllables and words. In fairly big words this can necessitate many fixations per word.

The most easily observable slow-reading defect is word-by-word reading. This is usually accompanied by finger pointing, the child's index finger indicating each word separately and thus narrowing the visual span to the width of only one word. Both word-by-word reading and eye wandering can be treated by providing the child with a reading window. This is a card the size of the page he is reading. Cut in it a slit the size of a line of print. The child puts the card on his page, reads through the window and slides the card down one space at the end of each line that he reads. Gradually increase the window depth to encompass two lines of print, and finally to three. When he can cope with a three-line window remove the card altogether. To prevent your pupil regressing to finger pointing at this stage get him to hold the book with both hands. Throughout this period of training keep the material simple so that your pupil is only dealing with one set of difficulties at a time, in this case visual ones.

Developing the intermediate reading skills

It is becoming customary to consider the course of reading growth as falling into three broad stages of skill development, as follows:

1 primary skills,
2 intermediate skills,
3 higher order skills.

Primary skills are those which the reader needs to enable him to discriminate between letter shapes and words and to achieve simple decoding. Intermediate skills are concerned with the development of speed and fluency, while the higher order skills are those which the skilled reader may draw on to satisfy almost every purpose in adult life. Higher order skills include study; locating, accessing and applying information; critical reading and appreciation.

Phrasing skills

One way to improve fluency is to organise effectively the material that is already there, so that words are grouped into meaning-clusters or phrases rather than separate words. This, in effect, is more than merely increasing visual span. It involves getting meaning from the span rather than just width. Note that some commercial speed-reading techniques concentrate on widening the visual span progressively without any attention to the acquisition of meaning. It cannot be overstressed that the purpose of reading is comprehension rather than mere speed.

Consider the two sentences below where the fixations are separated by diagonal lines.

(a) Peter / always / wears / blue / jeans, / check / shirts / and / desert / boots.

(b) Peter always / wears blue / jeans, check / shirts and / desert boots.

In sentence (b) there are only five fixations compared with the ten in sentence (a). The doubling of the visual span, as in sentence (b), has not made the sentence more easy to comprehend, rather the reverse has been the case.

The object of teaching phrasing skills is a two-fold one, namely both to improve comprehension and to increase reading rate – a real gain, that is, in overall reading efficiency. Sentence (c) below indicates an arrangement of the spans into four fixations which is likely to achieve these objectives: e.g.

(c) Peter always wears / blue jeans, / check shirts / and desert boots.

To teach your slow reader to read in phrases is not difficult. Look at sentence (c) above. You will note that a dot has been placed above the centre of each fixation. When you look at each dot your focus will rapidly widen so that as well as the dot you can see the words grouped below it. Beyond the fixation lines your vision is blurred. Do this with your pupil. Get a passage of reading matter which is at his independent level (even though he may, because of bad reading habits, only be able to read it word by word). Break the passage into phrases and mark them off by vertical lines as in sentence (c). Get your pupil to read the dots. In doing so he will read the phrases. Gradually increase the difficulty of the material until your prepared passages are at his instructional level.

Anticipation skills

The chances are that you, a competent adult reader, never remember even learning to read. It seems to many of us that reading is a thing that we have always been able to do, or at least had very little difficulty with ever. Probably you came from a home where the language background was sufficiently rich to give you a good start in school. When reading came, you probably had experience in speaking and listening of most of the common patterns of our language. Because of this facility, very early in the reading process you began to guess your way into reading rather than look at each letter or word. This is how you read now. You probably read at about 400 words a minute when you are reading your favourite novelist. This is eight words every second. If you read in the evening between seven and eleven o'clock you read about 100,000 words. Many of you can read many more than that. Obviously you haven't the time to look at every word, let alone every letter. You guess the greater part of them. You know this to be true because now and again you make the wrong guesses and then it dawns on you that you have completely lost the thread. Then you read back slowly and carefully until you are back on the right wavelength. Once there, imperceptibly you start speeding up until soon you are galloping away again at this guessing game called reading.

To show what a good guesser you are, complete the following story:

It was 8 a.m. Mary got up, went to the bathroom, got dressed, came downstairs and had . . . .

Did you supply the words 'her breakfast'? Good. Now read on and complete the story.

She put on her hat and coat, took her satchel, said good-bye, walked out to the crossing and asked the policeman . . . .

Did you supply 'to see her across the road'? The chances are that you completed both sentences with almost the identical words which I supplied myself. Note that these are quite sizeable chunks of language, two words in the first case and six in the second, and not merely a couple of letters or a single word. You were able to anticipate almost exactly the very words I was going to use because the words preceding them gave you the required mental set or direction. Another way of putting this is to say that some of my words started a certain pattern which you were able to complete. This is due to an aspect of language known as collocation, the

tendency of words to come together in fairly consistent groupings or patterns. Almost since birth you have been building up a stock of these patterns of language through speaking and listening and later through reading and writing. Your own personal stock of patterns enables you to anticipate many of the patterns and structures which appear both in speech and in print.

Note, however, that as soon as the expectations and language uses of reader and writer are not in harmony, anticipation becomes more difficult. Imagine that a writer is noted for setting up bizarre situations. Our 'story' could be slightly rewritten thus:

It was 8 a.m. Mary got up, went to the bathroom, got dressed, came downstairs and had A GAME OF LUDO WITH THE BUTLER.

The story continues:

She put on her hat and coat, took her satchel, said good-bye, walked out to the crossing and asked the policemen IF HE HAD A LIGHT FOR HER CIGAR.

Obviously we cannot anticipate the unexpected, which explains why you would not expect to see the words in capital letters, but rather 'her breakfast' and 'to see her across the road'. However with conventional and familiar material the ability to anticipate correctly saves us from actually reading and thus enables us to accomplish reading tasks at comparatively high speeds.

Not all children on starting school have acquired a repertoire of language patterns which enables them to anticipate structures likely to appear in print. If oral language development is not tackled with some thoroughness early in school, such children will be put on reading too soon. They will be asked to recognise words not yet in their experience, i.e. not cognised. If their language is very minimal almost every word could be unfamiliar. Lacking effective language patterns they have no basis for intelligent guessing or anticipation. They are therefore reduced to working out almost every word laboriously either by phonic analysis or by word shape clues, in which distinctive features like ascenders or descenders help them to identify the word. Either way they are reading letter by letter or word by word.

Some children do not develop anticipation skills because of the insistence on the part of their teachers on 100 per cent accuracy in oral reading. Imagine a teacher hearing her pupil read. He comes to the sentence:

He bought a present for his mummy.

The child reads:

He bought a present for his mother.

The pupil is about to read on when the teacher stops him. 'Wrong!' she says and points ominously to the word 'mummy'. 'Is that mummy or mother?' she asks.

The child is not really bothered because to him they both mean the same and he is anxious to get on with the story. The teacher insists on literal accuracy though both alternatives are semantically correct.

'Sound it out then,' she says, and proceeds to involve her pupil in the laborious process of phonic analysis to prove her point. By such ineptness teachers can thwart the natural tendencies of children to extract meaning from print in the most economical ways. The moral of this case study is that hearing children read can sometimes be overdone. Would not a more desirable alternative be occasionally to encourage children to guess? A further question is raised: can we be flexible enough to accept semantically accurate alternatives occasionally at the expense of literal exactitude?

Context as an aid to word recognition

The more quickly children can recognise words the more quickly and fluently they will read. There are three basic ways of identifying unfamiliar words. They are by:

1 phonic analysis
2 sight methods
3 using the context

Methods 1 and 2 are by far the most commonly used in Britain. Method 3 is rare. To show how the different methods work, consider the following case study.

You have a pupil reading aloud to you, thus: *Peter and Jane went to the circus.*
He stops after 'the' and waits for you to tell him the next word. You decide to put the onus on the pupil to work out the word and you opt for method 2, which is the method most British teachers would try first.
'What does it look like?' you ask.
Carrot, he says. *Peter and Jane went to the carrot.*
('Carrot' is the only word he can think of which approximates in shape and length to 'circus'.)
'Carrot?' you echo incredulously. 'How can Peter and Jane go to the carrot?'
'I don't know,' says your pupil.
Now you decide to try method 1. 'Well sound it out then,' you suggest.
The child does his best but his phonic skills are limited to a knowledge of the five short vowels and the single consonants. He has as yet only one sound value for 'c', which is the 'k' sound of the word 'cat'. He is also unaware of the extended vowel 'ir', also written as 'er' and 'ur'. He has not yet learned how to tackle digraphs. For him each letter signals a separate sound.
'Go on,' you say, 'sound it out.'
He sounds each letter in turn and says,
Ker-i-rah-ker-u-suh.
No matter how quickly you encourage him to

say the sounds they do not make the word 'circus'.

Finally you have a flash of inspiration.

'Forget that,' you say, 'and just read on.'

He starts again and reads, *Peter and Jane went to the* . . . . (he omits the unfamiliar word 'circus' and reads on). *They saw lions and tigers* . . . . Here he breaks off excitedly and says, 'I know the word. It's "zoo".'

'How do you know it's "zoo"?' you ask.

'Because that's where they keep lions and tigers,' he replies.

'O.K. Let's go back and see if that looks right,' you suggest.

He goes back, inspects the word and registers disappointment. 'No,' he says, 'it's not "zoo" Zoo is a little word. That word is bigger.'

'O.K.,' you say, 'then read on some more.'

He reads, *They saw lions and tigers and clowns.* 'Now I know the word. It's "circus". "Zoo" was wrong because there are no clowns there.'

Note how in this case the operation of primary skills (methods 1 and 2) only brings confusion. If you have slow readers to teach, give them plenty of practice in using the context. By doing this they use the words they already know in order to work out words which are unfamiliar.

Cloze procedure

Cloze procedure was devised by Taylor in 1953 as a means of measuring the readability of different newspapers. It is still being researched as a more general readability measuring device but recently has emerged as a most effective means of teaching the use of context cues and anticipation skills.

Briefly, the method involves the presentation of a text from which words have been deleted on a regular basis, e.g. every tenth word. Readers are invited to complete the blanks by examining the surrounding context and supplying suitable words. This activity is particularly enjoyable if the children work in groups on the blanks. Using this procedure, exercises to further the use of context can be programmed systematically and progressively. For example, more difficult activity results from increasing the frequency of the gaps, i.e. missing out more words. Work can be organised on a simpler basis for the *inept* reader by giving structure clues; e.g. the word 'cat' could be presented as a partial deletion, thus:

(shape clues only)

C (first letter and shape clues)

C _ _ (first letter and length clues)

_____ (context only)

There is a detailed discussion of the organisation of cloze procedure activities in my book, *Reading development and extension*, chapter 4.

For carefully graded children's exercises in developing context through the use of cloze procedure you might refer to those I prepared for *Read to think*, books 1, 2 and 3, published by Holmes McDougall. This series has been readability graded for reading ages 8·0–12·0 and the content is non-infantile. *The secondary remedial workshop*, published by Ward Lock Educational, contains graded cloze exercises suitable for slow readers in the secondary school. (See also cloze procedure as a means of testing and diagnosis, page 40 and as a way of assessing readability levels, page 87.)

Increasing reading rate

A further way to increase reading speed is to give practice in the use of timed exercises. Such activities feature prominently in the *SRA reading laboratories* and the Ward Lock *Reading workshops*. They are known as rate builders (SRA) and speed cards (Ward Lock) respectively. They consist of a number of carefully graded cards each of which contains a brief passage and a number of comprehension questions. Each card must be read and the questions answered in writing within a time limit of three minutes. The rate builders and speed cards are designed to develop the pupil's ability to

read faster,
concentrate on the reading,
understand the main ideas and supporting details quickly,
think clearly under time pressure.

The other main areas of the *SRA reading laboratories* and Ward Lock *Reading workshops* are named respectively *Power builders* and *Work cards*. Though these are concerned chiefly with the development of comprehension, vocabulary, word study and spelling the child is encouraged to tackle the work at the fastest rate possible. When the results of each exercise are recorded the time taken forms part of the record and the children are encouraged to beat the time-span of the previous exercise.

The *Swift reading scheme*, by Elder and Wood (published by Harrap) has five well-graded pupils' books in which the accent is on increasing reading rate. There is follow-up material to these in *Swifter reading practice* which is organised in three well-graded little books of from thirty-eight to forty-eight pages.

Summary

In this section I investigated verbalisation, inadequate focussing and inept phrasing as major causes of slowness of reading rate. Specific remediation for these defects was suggested. The importance of anticipation and the use of context was stressed and exercises in cloze procedure were recommended to develop these skills. Commercially produced materials specifically designed to accelerate reading rate were also introduced.

The reluctant reader

The reluctant reader is one who can read but doesn't. He has the ability but rarely puts it to use. When you spend much time and effort teaching children to read and at the end of it all find your attempts to develop the reading habit unrewarded by success, you may indeed question whether the effort is worth while. My own view is that there are, in fact, not so many reluctant readers at all. We have a highly literate population which uses reading for many purposes. The proof of this is in the number of books published annually. Each year more books are published than in any year before. What is probable is that less fiction is being read than used to be the case. This is understandable. Reading for pleasure has to compete with a host of attractions which new technology and increased leisure and affluence have made possible. Reading fiction was once a major pursuit when fewer forms of leisure were available and many teachers can remember immersing themselves in books in the not too distant past. It is easy for some of us therefore to confuse the reading of fiction with reading for pleasure and to view other purposes for reading as less satisfying. However, the man who spends his Sunday mornings tinkering under his car bonnet with the help of his car manual undeniably gets much pleasure from his reading. So does the housewife who successfully creates some new dish with the help of her cookery book. Perhaps then we should be more realistic about the amount of time people might devote to reading. It may be that we can best help our pupils by showing them that reading has many purposes and can take many forms, that reading fiction is just one form and possibly the escapism that often accompanies it is merely one purpose. The more purposes we have for reading the more we can live a satisfying life in a modern society and the more can reading be regarded as an essential tool for the living of a full life.

There are, indeed, some children who, even though they can read competently, would only use print as a means of satisfying needs as a last resort. There is likely to be more than one cause of such reluctance. Many reluctant readers had too early an introduction to books in infant school. For them the acquisition of literacy has been an uphill struggle all the way and associations with pleasure would be few. In many cases the teaching has concentrated on the acquisition of skills rather than the development of interests. Some reluctant readers read slowly. They take so long to get the point that they do not find all the effort involved worth the trouble. For them it is easier to ask for information than to find it themselves in books. The film is easier to watch than the book is to read. Some have not been encouraged to read widely either at home or at school and have not established a set of purposes which reading could satisfy if they chose to use it.

As a profession we have in the past paid lip-service to the idea that the development of the reading habit is a major aim in teaching reading. Unfortunately no significant body of teachers have regarded it as their concern. This is because reading has been confused with beginning reading – the job of the infant teacher. We are only just widely accepting the fact that reading is a developmental process which extends well into adulthood. Later stages of schooling have not capitalised on the start given us by the infant school. We have assumed that the width of the curriculum in middle and secondary schools would necessitate wider reading. We now know that this is not enough. If we want the reading habit to grow we have to set about organising systematically to achieve it.

There are certainly difficulties in the way. In order to encourage children to read we need to know them well, as persons as well as readers. We need an accurate knowledge of their needs, abilities and interests in order to give them appropriate reading matter. We need some knowledge of readability measurement so that they can read the books we recommend without undue difficulty. We need a knowledge of children's fiction so that we can give them up-to-date or relevant material. We know that reading fashions change over quite short spells of time and that books which appealed to us when we were young may not attract the young people of today. As well as all this knowledge, which takes considerable time to acquire, there is the problem of finding time to record this information in order that we may put it to use.

How have we faced up to these difficulties in the past? The short answer is – we haven't. What we have done has been generalised rather than specific; hopeful rather than purposeful. Our practices have tended to reinforce those who already have the reading habit. Such practices include library visits, the provision of class and school libraries, book fairs, book clubs, book readings, book reports and general exhortations to use these and other facilities offered. The habitual readers make use of these facilities. They would probably get books from other sources even if these avenues were not available. Those who have not developed the reading habit soon flag after a temporary spurt involving much effort on our part. They easily drop out and lose the impetus.

It is possible that the knowledge explosion itself of recent years has killed off the chances for many children of ever acquiring the reading habit. There is so much to know that the curriculum has widened out of all belief and we could not possibly teach it all. Consequently we have put the onus on the children to teach themselves, to find their own information and apply it in topics and projects. The result has been a concentration on the location and application of facts, using reading as a tool and not as a delight in its own right. There is little doubt that the reading of fiction has declined alarmingly in the middle and secondary schools during the last two decades.

To take a more positive view, we now need to consider new organisational procedures and teaching methods which are specifically designed to promote the reading habit.

Reading inventories

If you had to record the needs, interests and abilities of all your pupils you would have no time left for teaching them to read. So why not let your pupils record all this themselves? The method is simple. Wherever there are books (e.g. class libraries, school libraries or subject libraries) have piles of record cards easily available. Train and encourage your pupils every time they get a new book to take a new record card with it. Get them to write on the card, their name, the name and author of the book and the date the book was selected. On returning the book get them to write the date when it was returned, the number of pages read, and a comment on how interesting or enjoyable they found it. If books are selected out of school encourage the readers to complete record cards relating to these in school as soon as possible. The cards should be kept in a large envelope or other suitable container.

If these cards are completed thoroughly an accurate profile of the child's reading interests will gradually be compiled. It should be made clear to the child that the inventory will be looked at by you at least once every term. Make clear too that your inspection of the reading inventory will not be made in any punitive way but as a help in getting to know the reader's strengths and weaknesses in order to further his reading development. You should also point out that new books will be acquired on the basis of the interests and preferences stated on the record cards. My experience is that once children know that their teacher will look at their reading inventories regularly they tend to do more reading and to show this on their cards. Why should the more reluctant keep on reading if no one shows interest or gives them encouragement and support?

Reading interviews

The reading inventory is an even more potent promoter of the reading habit if it is organised with a reading interview in mind. Once a term collect each child's records and go over with him individually all he has read since his last interview. This will give you the opportunity to encourage him to read more as well as to congratulate him on what he has read so far. Don't rush the interview. Give the child time to tell you about the books and authors he has enjoyed as well as about the difficulties he has met. Suggest to him further reading either by the same or a similar author or on a similar theme. If it were possible to have one or both parents present with you and the child at the termly interview the whole business would be elevated almost to the level of a ceremony. Provided that the interview was conducted in a pleasant, encouraging way, this would be no mean thing. It would show the family that you and the school accord to reading and to the growth of the reading habit the highest possible status and importance. On such occasions you could also suggest to parents ways in which they could effectively play their part in encouraging their children to become habitual readers. You can be sure that the certainty that such an interview will occur will encourage most parents to concern themselves more about the reading their children do. On the other hand, if you don't show interest – why should they?

Finding time for reading interviews and inventories

Many schools now use *SRA reading laboratories* and Ward Lock *Workshops*. If you have experience in working with these materials you will know that with them the majority of children can work at their own level and their own pace for periods of from thirty minutes to an hour. It is on these occasions when all the class are busy at quiet individual work that you could most easily and profitably take two or three children in turn for their reading interviews. Periods such as these guarantee that you and your interviewees can be free from interruption and distraction. This is necessary if the interviews are to be conducted in an unhurried, enjoyable and encouraging manner.

For a detailed account of an actual reading interview case study I prepared one for *Reading development and extension*, chapter 8.

New methods of teaching the reading of fiction

We only form habits by doing things we enjoy. Middle and secondary pupils who have not acquired the reading habit have not been taught to read for enjoyment. We have taught them the skills of reading, but not its pleasures. In this case, let us alter our ways and give them reading experiences which are stimulating and enjoyable. Because of inept ways of teaching reading in the past many unwilling readers are passive, asking little of the text and its author. Past ways of teaching and testing comprehension have tended to support this passivity by concentrating on recall and recognition of detail at a purely literal level. The readers have neither been stretched nor involved.

What is needed is a change of attitude so that the passive reader becomes active and involved, challenging the author all the way by reading critically. How do we get such a reaction? By considering the reactions of the avid reader and organising so that these same reactions occur in the minds of the reluctant. The avid reader thinks of reading as a challenge. What keeps most readers reading to the end is the story line. This is the path which takes us from the beginning of the story to the end. There may be side-tracks but it is the ending which keeps us going from the very beginning. The author constantly drops clues about the direction in which he is going. Sometimes he drops false clues which obscure the outcome. The avid reader accepts the author's challenge to keep up with him. He forms hunches which enable him to 'tune in' on the author's wavelength. Sometimes the hunches are wrong and have to be re-formed. Fairly early on, the scene is set and the various possible outcomes are stated. By a process of reasoning and evidence-gathering, inadequate hunches are discarded and the more accurate hunches confirmed. Note that it is the forming of hunches (probabilities) and the testing of them out in the imagination which give the joy and the pleasure. If the reader merely wanted to know the outcome, the first thing he would do would be to look at the last chapter where all is revealed. Note that this is the last thing that most readers do. They see reading as forward-looking, anticipatory, predictive and would probably be furious if you told them the outcome when they were half-way through. They want to predict the outcome themselves. It is these reactions which we must reproduce in the reluctant reader.

Predicting outcomes

To reproduce such reactions select a short story at the instructional readability level of your reader. Put him in a group of readers of roughly equal ability. The optimum size of group recommended for this activity is about ten, with eight as the lowest limit and twelve as the maximum. Tell the group that they are going to be given a short story which they are to read silently. The story will be presented in instalments. They will be asked to predict the exact outcome of the story as soon as possible. They will formulate hypotheses, some of which will be discarded as new evidence unfolds. They must give reasons for what they say and to do this must produce evidence either from the text or from their own experience. Wild speculation, unsupported by textual evidence, should be discouraged. Members of the group must be free to drop hunches and adopt new ones in the light of superior reasoning. To control all this you must act as an impartial chairman, not leading the group in any way, perhaps summarising the main hunches from time to time and presenting a new instalment when the discussion possibilities of the previous one have been exhausted.

To give you some idea of the kinds of thinking and mental reactions involved in such work, try to predict as soon as possible the exact outcome of the story below. You would find it more interesting if a colleague or two joined in the activity, thereby introducing an element of mild competition and a wider range of possibilities to argue about. There are seven instalments.

THE INHERITANCE
Instalment 1
In July 1936 the Reds occupied the island for some twelve days, during which time they desecrated the cathedral and killed thirty of the nationalist militia. Almost all of these died instantly when a Communist shell hit the citadel guardroom point-blank. One of the thirty was Mariano Vaquer. By a strange chance, at the precise moment when Mariano died in the walled city his second son, Juanito, was born in the Vaquer farm some five kilometres away on the edge of the coastal plain. The Communist shell which ended Mariano's life also cut short a number of agonising speculations as

to whether his second child would be so unfortunate as to be a boy.

Think hard about what is likely to happen. All kinds of probabilities spring to mind. These could be narrowed down by considering the title, the time and the place in which the story is set. There are still many questions raised, for which there are as yet no answers. Why, for instance, should the second child be 'unfortunate' if a boy? The main question, though, is what is Juanito going to inherit. Have you formed your hunch about that? Or is there some other possibility?

Instalment 2
Now to understand the concern of the father as to the sex of his second child one needs at least a smattering of the island's laws relating to inheritance. Firstly, family property is morally tied to male descendants. The historical reason for such blatant sex discrimination is that in an island which has known invasion from Greek, Roman, Carthaginian, Arab, Corsair, and now Communist, the farmer has from time immemorial been accustomed to leaving his plough and picking up his sword in defence of his land. Secondly, in an island so small the law is concerned to avoid property division as much as possible. The 'hereu', the Heir, the eldest male child, gets the largest and best share of the family land. The other sons must share out the marginal, poor quality land and this almost invariably implies a career away from the land and often far from the homeland itself. Sons who are not first-born emigrate to America or Algiers, stay at home and become priests or start on the ground floor in a military career.

Have you found here confirmation for your first hunch? Have you read something which caused you to change it? Is the outcome still 'inheritance'? Is the word 'unfortunate' from instalment

I now explained? If you are reading this with colleagues, what do they think?

Instalment 3
From the moment when his wife's second pregnancy was confirmed Mariano Vaquer had secretly hoped for a daughter. Such an outcome would eliminate any possible friction between brothers, one of whom would be seen to be remarkably favoured by a mere accident of birth. A daughter could look forward to a substantial dowry and was guaranteed by the island's law not only the right of lodging, but also, in return for certain services, the use of the family oven, kitchen and well. In effect, if a daughter remained unmarried the law ensured her the grant of an independent home as protection against the threat of exclusion from the soil in which she was born by too strict an interpretation of the laws of male primogeniture. Alas, such an outcome was not to be. Mariano died, Juanito was born, Nationalist troops landed and ended the brief period of Communist rule by machine-gunning the entire Red garrison and throwing their bodies over the city walls into the harbour approaches. The island has been staunchly Nationalist ever since.

What are the main hunches now? What evidence is there for these? If you are working with colleagues, what evidence can you find to refute their viewpoints?

Instalment 4 (the half-way point in the story)
The widow Vaquer did not re-marry. With the help of her father and brothers she managed the farm until her sons could take over, harvesting in due season oranges and lemons, almonds, olives, carobs and figs, and planting and pulling greens, root crops and potatoes twice a year, and hay, in good years, three times. Ramon, Mariano's 'hereu', grew up to take his responsibilities as hereu seriously. Only in high summer when the tempera-ture topped 100° did he stop for a brief siesta. The rest of the year he worked in the fields from dawn to dusk. In the cool of the evening he then fed the pigs, milked the cows and goats and mucked out the stables. By the time he had reached his majority he could manage the farm single-handed, providing he spent most of the time working and devoted only a minimum of time to eating and sleeping. It was perhaps as well, at least for the fortunes of the Vaquer farm, that Ramon could and did work so hard.

This is the first detailed reference to Ramon. Has this changed your hunches in any way? Can you now confidently predict the exact outcome of the story?

Instalment 5
At forty the widow Vaquer had grown so fat that cooking, washing and other household tasks were as much as she could manage. There was no possibility of her helping with the general work of the farm. As for Juanito, his interest in farming declined abruptly on his thirteenth birthday. It was then that his mother, panting heavily in her peasant black and shiny with sweat despite the constant use of her fan, took Juanito on a tour of the farm at nine in the morning when the temperature was already in the eighties. She pointed out that Ramon as the eldest son was the 'hereu' and she showed Juanito all the 'hereu's' lands. These were flat and well irrigated for arable use or nicely terraced and planted out with various fruit trees at the higher levels. She then showed Juanito the land assigned to him. This was on the seaward side of the holding and consisted mainly of bare rock fronting abruptly on to the sea with a stand of low pines atop. The timber, said Juanito's mother, could be sold when he came of age to help him set up in business or buy a parcel of land of better quality elsewhere on the island. Meanwhile, she continued, Juanito should be considering a career.

The story has now swung back from Ramon to Juanito. What will happen to him?

Instalment 6
On and off for three years Juanito considered career
possibilities and earned his keep by tending his
brother's sheep and goats. Only for brief periods did
his flocks feed in the better lands, cropping the
stubble left after the hay harvests. Most of the time
both he and they sought the shade of the pines and
the cool breezes which frequently fanned the rocks on
the higher land which belonged to him. The work
was not onerous. Juanito let his flocks graze on
fragrant shoots of thyme and sage, juniper and
marjoram and only discouraged them with a deftly
thrown stone when they showed intentions of
attacking his young pines. On days when even the
shade became too hot he would strip off his clothes
and trot naked down to the beach and fall into the
sea. There, floating lazily, he would survey his
patrimony through half-closed eyes. Sometimes
while thus engaged he would hear his brother in the
fields beyond roundly cursing his mule and urging
it to keep the plough straight. At such moments the
thought crossed Juanito's mind that the 'hereu's'
lot is not necessarily a happy one. And at one such
moment he decided on his future career.

You are probably thinking by now that Juanito
is not at all keen to inherit the farm. Bearing in
mind the title and the insights gained from the
above instalment about Juanito's attitudes, it
seems likely that he will make the best use of
what he has. So, what will be do?

Final instalment
The first stage of this involved a period of appren-
ticeship. Like many Vaquers before him Juanito
too emigrated. He was, however, the first Vaquer to
work in England as a waiter. He came to sympa-
thise with his English clients on their cold grey
skies and bleak climate and soon realised why the
English fling off their clothes at the merest hint of
sunlight. It is a phenomenon with which they have
slight acquaintance. One day he discussed these

matters with a client who disclosed that he owned
the large hotel where Juanito worked. A friendship
formed. On his twenty-first birthday Juanito sold a
half-share of his patrimony in exchange for a
half-share in the hotel which the English hotelier
built upon it. It was the first tourist hotel built by
foreign capital in Ibiza and it was not the last.
Juanito alone is said to own eighteen. He is also
said to have started a revolution, for these days the
'hereus' sell off their coastal lands for property
development while their luckless younger brothers
work the good lands from dawn to dusk.

Whether your hunches were accurate or not, you
would probably agree that the challenge to
predict the outcome made you read with greater
commitment than you would normally bring to
the reading of a short story. The commitment
would be greater if you were a member of a
reading group and had to give evidence for your
point of view as well as finding counter-evidence
for the views of other participants. It is the
thinking, reasoning element in this activity
which generates the questioning attitudes which
characterise the critical reader.

Organising prediction activities
As with reading interviews you would probably
choose to take a group for prediction work when
the rest of the class are working on reading
laboratories or workshops. The main thing is to
match the reading matter to the group. Brighter
readers need fairly difficult material to stretch
them. Poorer groups need simpler texts. Very
often the best material is that which children
write themselves. There are likely to be fewer
readability problems with such material than
with that written for children by adults.
    The material is most easily presented by
writing each instalment on a transparency and
projecting it on to a screen with an overhead
projector. In time a stock of transparencies can

be built up to suit the needs and interests of most reading groups. Alternatively, books of short stories could be used. You would need a book for each child and one for yourself. Open the books at the page where your story starts. Trap this double page (instalment 1) between two elastic bands one at each of the outer edges of each book. As each instalment is discussed and its possibilities exhausted slide the next page through the bands.

Prediction work can be made progressive by starting on very short stories which gradually increase in length. In time whole books could be tackled, chapter by chapter.

Motivational value of prediction activities

You will note that in the above activity no writing was done by the participants, that is – by you and your colleagues. This would certainly be so when working with children. In almost all other reading exercises you can think of being tackled in school, writing is an inevitable concomitant. Many children are discouraged from reading by the certainty that written exercises will follow. Much of this writing can be of considerable duration especially when the reading leads to the development of projects and extended topics. In the case of a typical prediction exercise the whole thing is started, enjoyed and finished within, say, half an hour. It is hoped that by short sharp bursts of teaching activity such as this you can bring enjoyment and variety to the reading lesson.

Summary

In this chapter the motivational role of reading interviews and inventories in fostering the reading habit was stressed. Outcome prediction was considered as a means of challenging readers to become actively, critically (and pleasurably) involved in the act of reading.

The competent reader
Developing comprehension

In Britain the traditional emphasis in teaching reading has been at beginning or remedial level. It was something small children learned to do in infant schools and consolidated later with little organised or directed help from teachers. If this didn't happen we started all over again and called it remedial reading. Recently it is being more generally recognised that each successive stage of schooling makes increased demands on reading competence. We are also more aware that few readers improve sufficiently to meet greater demands simply by a process of maturation. Few will improve without good teaching. One of the goals of schooling must be to prepare our children to face the demands of adult life and in this respect reading has a major role to play. The more those of you who teach the ten- to sixteen-year-olds accept responsibility for their reading development the more will you be concerned that they acquire the higher order skills. Chief among these is comprehension and from the teacher's point of view the most important fact about it is that you *can* teach it. You do not have to wait for it to come.

In order to teach comprehension you have to know what it is. The problem of definition is that it is not just one thing, i.e. understanding. It appears to be a complex of different levels of understanding in a hierarchical progression. Though there is often much overlap between categories five broad bands are discernible:

1 *Literal*
A simple surface level where the words mean just what they say. To answer a question at this level you would lift words straight from the text.
2 *Reorganisational*
Still a surface level but the words must be reorganised in some way to produce the meaning required.

3 Inferential

Here the meaning is not actually stated but implied. To understand at this level you have to read between the lines.

4 Evaluatory

At this level the reader is called upon to weigh the pros and cons of what is said in order to make a judgment on the basis of evidence either stated or implied.

5 Appreciative

Here the reader makes an emotional response to the text, e.g. feels awe, fear, dread, relief, excitement, etc., or shows an awareness of the author's command of language by an appreciation of style, diction and imagery.

In the past we have tended to test comprehension mainly at the literal level and a glance at sets of traditional comprehension exercises will show that questions are usually of this kind. There are two reasons for this. They are the easiest to set and the easiest to mark. Consider the passage below:

Poor Fred! On Saturdays Fred goes to the match. He sits in the unreserved seats in the Stretford end. He stays in every night amid a tempest of sound from his stereo, reading his favourite papers, Melody Maker *and* New Musical Express. *Poor Fred! He is tone deaf. He can't read a note and is devoid of musical talent. And yet in dreams he sees his name in lights. He has a rare gift for numbers has Fred. He can see order and pattern in numbers where to you and me there is only chaos. We take hours to work out with much labour what Fred sees in a flash. Alas, this great gift lies unused, red with the rust of apathy. I can see poor Fred some years from now in some dark cul-de-sac of mute frustration, like so many of his generation, his talents atrophied, with no dreams left.*

You will find it very simple to set any amount of level 1 (literal) questions on this passage: e.g.

What is the name of the boy in the passage? (Fred)
What day does Fred go to the match? (Saturday)
Which seats does Fred sit in?   (unreserved)

You will also note that little mental activity is required to pick out the answers straight from the text. For this reason this type of comprehension question is often termed 'nit-picking'.

Level 2 questions, involving a reorganisation of what is explicitly stated in the text, are harder to set. They often call for a paraphrase or summary, e.g.
How many favourite papers has Fred?   (two)
Note that the information – '*Melody Maker* and *New Musical Express*' – required to answer the question is in the text but has to be presented as a number. It is still a literal response.

Can you think up some level 2 questions? Ask a colleague to comment critically on their quality.

The answers to level 3 (inferential comprehension) questions cannot be found directly in the text. To find them you have to use clues in the text which enable you to 'put two and two together', e.g.
What kind of music does Fred like?   (pop)
Which football team does Fred support? (Manchester United)
Note that to make the above inferences we need to bring previous knowledge and experience to bear on the textual clues '*Melody Maker* and *New Musical Express*' and 'Stretford end'.

Try out on a colleague some questions on the passage which will lead him to draw inferences or implications.

Level 4 questions require the reader to make a judgment or critical evaluation of what he has read. He would be expected to give evidence in support of what he says, e.g.

The author blames Fred's failure to use his ability on his love for pop music. Say whether you agree or disagree with this view, giving reasons for your answer.

Such questions are difficult to frame, particularly with a view to eliminating the possibility of one-word answers, e.g. 'yes' or 'no'. Either response might be satisfactory if one were asked: 'Do you think the author is right in taking such a view?'

You will agree that this type of question is difficult to set. It would be even more difficult to mark. The number of reasons and the quality of the reasoning would make some answers better than others, yet all could be 'right'.

Below are my attempts to produce a level 5 response, i.e. an emotional reaction or one which indicates an appreciation of the author's style. You will notice that these are much more wordy than anything at previous levels. This is because of the difficulty I experienced in eliminating possible responses which could be evaluatory rather than appreciative.

Either (a) If you agree with the author that Fred is an object of pity, imagine Fred at age forty. Describe his job, home circumstances, relationships, attitudes towards life and other people.
Or (b) Comment critically on how well you think the author achieves his objectives by his use of:

(i) tempest of sound
(ii) red with the rust of apathy
(iii) some dark cul-de-sac of mute frustration.

The comprehension triangle

Despite the apparent complexity of the above questions there is no guarantee that they will result in comprehension at the levels required. This is because they take no account of the potential reader at whom they are directed. Comprehension is the result of the interaction of three ingredients, the reader, the text and the questions, and can perhaps be most easily visualised thus:

Questions alone, no matter how good, will not produce comprehension. They have to have a reader or readers in mind. If the reader lacks experience or ability he cannot comprehend. For example, I know of more than one eminent professor of English Literature who is not keen on football and who has never heard of the Stretford end. Such a person would not therefore be able to answer the apparently simple question above (level 2): 'Which football team does Fred support?' In this case not only does the question present the reader with an impossible task, this part of the text is too difficult for the professor (with his particular experience or lack of it) to understand.

Some texts are so simple that it is impossible to see in them levels of meaning other than the merely literal. If we are to develop comprehension in our pupils we must take account of their reading experience and ability and progressively introduce them to texts of gradually increasing complexity and levels of meaning. Here your ability then to set the right questions is crucial. If you only pose questions at literal levels you will only be developing literal comprehension.

So far you have been observing my attempts

to frame a range of comprehension questions on a text aimed at yourselves – the readers, whom I must vaguely categorise 'intelligent adults'. Why not have a try yourselves?

Select a passage suitable for reading instruction for a child for whom you are responsible. Devise a range of questions, say ten, that is two at each of the five major levels. Pencil in alongside each question a brief extract to indicate the area in the text which you expect your reader to use in order to answer the question. Give your reader a copy of the text and of the questions. Sit with your pupil and write down the responses he gives. Unless you have exceptional flair and insight you will probably find that once the literal levels are disposed of, the questions you devised will not always lead to the textual area you expected. That is, they will not lead to the level of comprehension that you wanted. In order to lift your pupil to that level you will probably have to ask additional questions.

Repeat this activity with a pair of children using the same materials. Let them work together discussing each question and the most appropriate strategies for answering it. Write down their responses. You will probably find that in order to answer correctly they will have had to formulate for themselves some of the additional questions you found it necessary to supply to help the child working on his own.

Now try the same exercise with a group of about twelve children. Give each child a copy of the text and ask the questions orally. Allow each child opportunities to give the answer he thinks best and to give reasons for his choice. If there is disagreement, encourage the children to decide by evidence and superior reasoning why one alternative is ultimately correct. You will probably find the children setting all sorts of questions for each other on the way and there will be no need for you to do anything but chair the discussion and keep it within bounds. I hope you will find

as a result of these brief experiments that the best and most enjoyable way to develop comprehension is by group discussion based on silent reading.

Finally, I hope you will forgive me for making one or two points which are obvious to most of you, if not quite all.

● Encourage the children to read the questions first. They will then have a purpose for reading and the questions themselves will cause them to decide on the most appropriate reading strategies, rather than coming to the reading cold.

● Always allow the children access to the text as well as the questions. Not infrequently the testing of comprehension is confused with memory training – e.g. 'Close your books then answer these questions.'

● Comprehension exercises frequently have a punitive aura – e.g. 'Now we'll see how well you've done your reading by the way you answer these questions.' If the whole thing can be made enjoyable, the pupils seeing themselves more as detectives challenged to solve problems, with more discussion and less writing, and working in groups rather than on their own, comprehension could yet be fun to do and fun to teach.

Commercially produced 'comprehension' materials

There are many sets of traditional comprehension exercises still on the market but they have been in bad odour for some time because of the trivial literal levels at which they are organised.

SRA have made commendable efforts to raise the level of questioning and to devise texts capable of being comprehended at higher levels. Some of the multiple-choice questions are particularly searching. Though the levels in the lower reading laboratories are as literal as anything on the market, Labs 2A, B and C, 3A, B and C, and 4A are excellent. The '2' labs are aimed at competent readers in the middle

Musical Allsorts

A stout man with a pink face wears
dingy white flannel trousers, a blue coat
with a pink handkerchief showing, and a
straw hat much too small for him, perched
5 at the back of his head. He plays the
guitar. A little chap in white canvas
shoes, his face hidden under a felt hat like
a broken wing, breathes into a flute; and a
tall thin fellow, with bursting over-ripe
10 button boots, draws ribbons – long,
twisted, streaming ribbons – of tune out of
a fiddle. They stand, unsmiling but not
serious, in the broad sunlight opposite the
fruit-shop; the pink spider of a hand beats
15 the guitar, the little squat hand, with a
brass and turquoise ring, forces the
reluctant flute, and the fiddler's arm tries
to saw the fiddle in two.

Katherine Mansfield

Another Fabulous Musician

For Discussion

1. In the piece "Musical Allsorts", where did the writer see the three musicians?

2. Why do you think they were there? What do we call people who do this?

3. Which instrument did each man play?

4. Were they good musicians? Towards the end of the passage the writer hints whether they were good musicians or not. Consider each man in turn and say which hint tells you about his musical talent.

5. "ribbons – long, twisted, streaming ribbons" (lines 10–11). Why does the author use these words to describe the fiddler's sounds?

6. Think of a word or a short phrase which you believe best describes how the men appeared. Don't use funny or strange or odd.

7. Why do you think that the men are dressed as they are?

8. Which of the players did the author notice most? Why do you think this was so?

9. "They stand unsmiling but not serious" (line 12). If they were neither smiling nor grim, describe how they did look.

10. Do you think that they were likely to be successful or unsuccessful in their 'jobs'? Why do you think so?

years while the '3' labs plus lab 4A would stretch most readers in the upper reaches of secondary school.

Holmes McDougall have produced two sets of children's texts and exercises suitable for the junior and middle years. *Scope for reading*, in three well-graded books, uses a variety of extracts as the starting point for group and individual work aimed at developing the whole range of comprehension skills. *Read to think*, also in three books, aims mainly at developing reorganisational and inferential skills. All books give carefully graded exercises in sequencing skills and are all graded progressively for readability. There are also exercises in word study, using context and outcome prediction. All the activities in *Read to think* are intended to be used on group discussion lines.

Thematic approaches to teaching reading

Thematic approaches make it possible to capitalise on an interest shared by most of the children as a starting point for further reading, writing and other activities. The success of these approaches depends on your ability to organise varied work and give all children opportunities to participate and make useful contributions. Much teaching in middle and secondary schools in subjects like English, History, Geography and Religion is thematic and is, in effect, a reading lesson. The children all read some common text, discuss it and answer questions on it.

The class lesson

Nowadays, when mixed ability classes are becoming increasingly fashionable, whole class methods are rightly out of favour. Even in tightly streamed classes there is great variation in interests and ability between the poorest and the ablest children. The main weaknesses of class methods are that all pupils are expected to read the same material whether it interests them or not and there is scant attention to individual differences. Bearing these weaknesses in mind, and there is little doubt that mass methods have been overdone, the class lesson still remains the most obvious and economical means of introducing the theme and generating work on it.

Organising the class reading lesson

● The main difficulty is in selecting the material to be read. It would need to have exceptionally high interest value to interest an entire class. Readability levels would need to be low enough not to frustrate the poorer readers yet not so simple as to bore the ablest.

● By appropriate questioning, ascertain the children's previous knowledge. Build on relevant experiences to bring them to the most suitable starting point.

● Having previously noted hard words and unfamiliar concepts which may cause difficulty, introduce these to the children in suitable contexts before they meet them in print.

● Build up expectation and interest by high-lighting some striking incident or information which bears closely on the theme.

● Now let the children start the first reading silently. Don't let them read in a vague, purpose-less way. Make sure they have pencils and notebooks and give them some positive directions as to what to read, e.g. noting difficult vocabulary, summarising in sequence the main details, writing in their own words the main idea, etc. The first reading should be fairly rapid and give the readers a good idea of the skeleton or basic organisation of the reading matter.

● Having cleared up any difficulties arising from the first reading, now get the children to read the text again. As before give clear directions as to the purpose of the reading, e.g. character studies, evaluation of conclusions or credibility of outcomes, answering comprehension questions.

● Correct major errors by further questioning. Discuss alternative answers.

Note. This method would be much more effective if the text were written at two levels, one for below average readers and one for average and above. The children could then be divided into two or three groups and be matched to different activities according to ability. The below average groups would not be expected to tackle all the activities.

Working with groups

If the two or three major groups referred to in the note above were divided into sub-groups (the number would depend on how many you could cope with effectively) much greater variety of work could be undertaken. The variety could be increased if the sub-groups were rotated from activity to activity in subsequent lessons. Many of my second-year college of education students have organised thematic reading periods very well using the following system based on six ability groups.

Group 1 Vocabulary
Task:
(a) lists hard words
(b) finds these in dictionaries
(c) checks possible meanings against context
(d) writes on board words and suitable meanings

Group 2 Individual work
Task: Members work individually on writing activities from workcards prepared by teachers.

Group 3 Audio/visual
Task: Members compile resource bank of supporting material from record, tape and film-strip catalogues, also pictures and cuttings from library.

Group 4 Art
Task: Illustrates hard words and phrases, characters and situations, and makes cartoons or collages to trace major sequences.

Group 5 Drama
Task: Chooses passages for miming or unscripted plays. Makes simple props and costumes.

Group 6 Reference
Task: Works under Librarian, cross-referencing material from related texts. Presents this to class in short reports.

Note While the six sub-groups are busy the teacher works with the remedial group on specialised activities.

Using multi–level reading schemes

Multi-level materials are so called because they enable children of different abilities to work at their own individual level. The Ward Lock *Reading workshop, 9–13* is aimed at children in middle school. SRA have seven reading laboratories suitable for competent readers in the age range ten to sixteen. The distinctive features of these materials are as follows:

● By testing, each child's correct starting point is ascertained. He goes on from there to learn new skills at his own pace.

● The work is carefully programmed into learning steps of gradually increasing difficulty. This gentle gradient encourages the readers to aim at and achieve increasingly high standards.

● The children record thoroughly all their work as soon as it is finished and corrected. The recording is a powerful motivator as it encourages readers to compete with their own best performances rather than against other children.

● The children themselves are trained to undertake many administrative tasks such as marking, correcting, recording, which are normally performed by teachers. Thus the responsibility for making progress is placed on the child himself.

● There is immediate feedback which few approaches can rival. Errors are detected and corrected by the children themselves almost as soon as they are made. There is no over-learning or reinforcement of errors as often occurs when children have to wait for long periods to have their work marked by teachers.

● Extremely varied content and readability progressions are built in to foster improvement in vocabulary growth, comprehension and reading speed.

Reading laboratories and workshops

A typical *SRA reading laboratory* has three sections: *Power builders, Rate builders* and *Listening builders*. Ward Lock *Reading workshops* have *Work cards* and *Speed cards* but no listening section.

Power builders

These consist of 150 cards divided into 10 sets of 15 each. Each set is colour coded and the cards in each colour band are of equal difficulty. Each *Power builder* is a four-page folder and contains:

An attractively illustrated title.
A passage of text. These increase in length and difficulty at each successive level.
Exercises in vocabulary, word study and comprehension based on the passage.

Power builders are designed to:
(a) develop comprehension;
(b) give practice in finding the main idea;
(c) detect the author's purpose;
(d) improve vocabulary and spelling.
There is an answer card for each *Power builder*.

Rate builders

These parallel the *Power builders* in 10 colour coded sets of 15 cards. Each contains a brief text and some comprehension questions. The text has to be read and the questions answered in writing within three minutes. The purpose of the *Rate builders* is discussed on page 56.

Listening builders

These consist of 10 exercises in the teachers' handbook. They are designed to give children practice in listening carefully and remembering what they hear. The teacher reads each one to groups or individuals who answer questions on the passage.

Organising multi-level work in the classroom

● Each child is given a reading test, the results of which you record in his record book. You convert his test score to a colour score with the help of a chart in your teachers' handbook.

● It takes about a week to familiarise the children with the organisation of the record books in which all work is written, corrected and evaluated. When they can do this on practice assignments set them to work on their appropriate colour assignments.

● When a child completes a *Power builder* and its parallel *Rate builder* he corrects and evaluates his work and graphs the result on charts in the record book.

● When his graphs indicate that his work is consistently good, e.g. 85 per cent or more on four or five consecutive cards, promote the child to the next colour level.

Advantages of SRA work

The material has high interest value and really caters for individual differences. The material is compact and easy to use and to store. The *Pilot libraries* which accompany the kits extend reading from cards into books and then into the use of school and community library facilities. There is a thorough and systematic treatment of the major skills of reading. Treated as a one-term crash course, which is what its designers recommend, it is usually successful in raising average reading ages by one year in the space of twelve weeks. In addition to this intrinsic merit, reading laboratories occupy the children gainfully for periods of up to one hour and thus free you to work with groups or individuals on a wide range of other reading, writing and speaking activities.

Reading for understanding

SRA also produce three RFU (reading for understanding) kits, which are particularly suitable for competent readers aged ten to sixteen. They are designed to encourage reading/thinking skills including sequencing and making logical judgments. The three editions are designated Junior, General and Senior and are aimed respectively at age groups 9–14, 11–16 and 14–18.

Study and reference skills

The SRA *Researchlab* saves busy teachers and librarians devising practice material in library and research skills. It is recommended for pupils between nine and fifteen years of age.

71

Study skills

In primary schools one of the main preoccupations of small children is learning to read. In secondary schools the emphasis is reversed and the focus is on reading to learn. We cannot be complacent about the help we have given children in this respect in the past. Too often it has been incidental. We have known too little about it to be able to offer effective direct teaching. Nowadays we can be more confident than we have been because we are aware that skills can be taught provided that the teaching is organised in a systematic way. We are fortunate also in being able to draw on the considerable expertise which has been developed in the United States where a number of study systems have been tried and tested. Of these, SQ3R, which was developed in the first place by F. P. Robinson, is probably the best known. It is one which the SRA Reading Laboratories apply to all their assignments and I think they are wise in this as SQ3R involves fewer stages than most other systems.

Study is quite a different activity from reading. Reading leads to forgetting. The purpose of study is to help us to remember what we find so that we may apply the knowledge gained and put it to use. Study therefore involves a number of stages additional to that of reading in that information is sought for a definite purpose, located, understood, stored (if need be) and applied, possibly at some later date. Study is a purely utilitarian skill and in teaching it we should aim to show children how to get knowledge and use it with the least possible effort and in the shortest possible time.

Teaching SQ3R

SQ3R involves five stages: surveying, questioning, reading, reviewing and reciting. In this connection 'reciting' means 'proving to oneself',

i.e. testing. In the first place the strategies appropriate to each stage should be taught separately. With practice the student should integrate these strategies into a systematic attack on print.

Surveying

When you survey a text you read only those parts of a text which give you most meaning in the shortest possible time. You ignore those parts where unimportant details only are considered. Practice in surveying can best be given on group discussion lines as was recommended when organising for predicting outcomes. Give each member a copy of the text, say a chapter or an article, to be read silently but give them only half a minute to get as much of the most important information as they can. By discussion it will be revealed that those who were most successful were those who concentrated on certain areas which will be generally agreed to be:

the title;
the illustrations;
the first sentence
(or possibly the first paragraph);
the last paragraph.

There should be thorough discussion on ways in which each of these areas might be treated systematically and why, so that in time students habitually refer to these when confronted with new material.

Questioning

The purpose of the survey is to enable the reader to pick up the most important clues which enable him to 'tune in' accurately on the author's wavelength in the shortest possible time. In doing the survey, questions will automatically spring into the reader's mind, e.g.

What do I already know about this subject?
Why is the title phrased in such a way?

Where is the evidence for this conclusion?
What do the illustrations tell me about the characters, situations, periods, etc., of the story?
Are the conclusions facts, or merely the author's own opinions?

When questions such as these are set up in the mind the reader is not passive. He is motivated to read hard to find the answers. If the questions which the children themselves raise are brought out for discussion, they will often be more pertinent to their own needs than those which you might devise for them.

Reading

The group should then read the text silently to seek answers to their self-imposed questions. At this time, observe the group at work and make notes on the different kinds of reading styles which will be manifested. Some children will read smoothly, others will read in a jerky fashion, turning back or going ahead. Get the children to infer and discuss what different readers were doing by reading in different ways. Discuss the fact that some ways may be better for a particular purpose. Encourage the readers to try different reading strategies.

Within the group, differences in reading speed will be readily observable. Discuss the reasons for such differences. It may be possible to identify children whose slowness in reading is due to some remediable defect. If this is so, action on the lines suggested in the section 'The slow reader' could be undertaken. The readers should be led to discuss the importance of speed in reading: e.g., is the fastest reader in the group the best reader? From such discussions the point should emerge that the quality of the reading is the major concern, i.e. those who read well are good readers but those who read well and quickly are better. Having made the point that

comprehension must not be sacrificed for speed, encourage flexibility of reading speed. Some parts of the text may be simpler than others. The better readers probably noticed these parts and made a conscious decision to speed up and give them more superficial treatment than more difficult sections. These same readers would probably devote more time and effort to the difficult passages, whereas the poorer, more inflexible reader reads all passages, whether hard or easy, at the same rate.

Reviewing and reciting

In teaching study skills I have found it useful to leave a gap (preferably a full week) between the reading stage and the reviewing stage of SQ3R. This makes very clear to the group how inefficient is reading alone, despite the thoroughness with which it was done a mere week earlier. Much forgetting will probably have taken place and it is thus fairly easy to make the point that further stages are essential to reinforce and consolidate previous learning. The purpose of reviewing is to discover gaps in the learning and then learn those parts well. How thoroughly reviewing is done will depend on the purpose which the reader brings to the task. The student who is reading for an important examination on which his future career will depend, the father who is contemplating an expensive family holiday abroad, will be motivated to get every scrap of relevant knowledge from textbooks and brochures respectively. We cannot guarantee this kind of motivation with younger children in school and therefore some extrinsic motivation will generally be found to be necessary. Basic to good reviewing techniques are the skimming/scanning abilities. When skimming you only take directions from the print which act as signposts indicating 'Not here – read on'. By such minimal clues we home in on the areas where the important information is which we are seeking. Then we slow down (scan) and read it well. Many children, laboriously trained to read smoothly in a left-to-right direction, do not take readily to skimming and scanning. You would probably best build in extrinsic motivation and give practice in skimming and scanning by setting the readers questions which lead them to research the text in every major part. If your questions cover the whole range of comprehension levels, so much the better. Other ways of reviewing are to set essays, to get the children to write summaries or outlines, to present reports or lecturettes or to set questions of their own for other children to answer. This kind of work is most productive when the children work at it in pairs or small groups on discussion lines. The testing (reciting) and reviewing stages overlap considerably, as poor comprehension revealed by testing would indicate the need for further reviewing until the learning is achieved at a satisfactory level.

Summary

In this section I discussed the nature of comprehension and five different levels of comprehension. The importance of teachers' questions to develop comprehension was emphasised. There was some discussion of thematic approaches to developing reading and how classes may be organised with these in mind. The use of multi-level materials was reviewed. SQ3R was recommended as a study system particularly suitable for ten- to sixteen-year-olds.

Record keeping

Nearly all teachers agree about the need to keep adequate records of their pupils' progress. Good records should help pupils to improve in reading and should also be a help to the teacher, to parents and to other teachers, e.g. the teacher who will have your class next year. Records should indicate each child's reading level, identify strengths and weaknesses and evaluate progress. During the middle and secondary stages of schooling it is possible to record so many facets of schooling that recording could become a full-time occupation leaving little time for teaching. The task should not become a burden to you or take up time which might be better spent in teaching. It is up to each school staff to have a clear and realistic policy on this question by deciding what kinds of records they consider it essential to keep and to use those as well as is possible. Consequently I can do little more than suggest some of the kinds of records that may be suitable for different purposes or at different levels.

Recent ideas on recording are moving away from lists of marks, which are arbitrary and subjective, towards the use of checklists which have diagnostic as well as evaluative possibilities. These can be applied to any important area in reading and may be either negative or positive. The negative checklist lists common weaknesses and these are ticked off when particular defects have been remedied to a satisfactory level. The motivation checklists and oral reading faults checklist on the next few pages are of this kind. They are obviously of more use at remedial level than at any other.

Individual motivation checklist

Here are listed the more general factors contributing to backwardness. The purpose is to highlight the major areas of difficulty so that remediation can be relevant and specific.

By a change of format it is possible to record such details for a group or an entire remedial class as in the Class motivation checklist on page 76. Note how your reading of the separate factors is facilitated by setting the spaces in which they are written at an angle.

MOTIVATION CHECKLIST		
Name		
Date of birth		
Class		
Teacher		
Defect	**Action taken**	**Comments**
<u>Poor attitude</u>		
(i) No interest in in reading		
(ii) Indifferent		
(iii) Positive dislike of reading		
<u>Emotional factors</u>		
(i) Maladjustment		
(ii) Home conflicts		
(iii) Withdrawal		
(iv) Aggression		
<u>Physical factors</u>		
(i) Poor vision		
(ii) Poor hearing		
(iii) Poor speech		
(iv) Poor coordination		
(v) Left-handedness		
(vi) Other factors		

CLASS MOTIVATION CHECKLIST	Factors contributing to backwardness													
Class .... Teacher	No interest	Indifferent	Hates reading	Maladjustment	Home problems	Withdrawn	Aggressive	Poor vision	Poor hearing	Poor speech	Poor co-ordination	Left-handedness		
Pupils														Comments

76

ORAL READING FAULTS CHECKLIST		
Name		
Date of birth		
Class		
Teacher		
Defect	**Action taken**	**Comments**
Word by word reading		
Omission		
Substitution		
Addition		
Reversal		
Eye wandering		
Guessing		
Repetition		
Improper phrasing		
Disregard of punctuation		
Inept phonic analysis		
Inept syllabification		
Finger pointing		

Records such as the one on page 71 enable you to identify specific weaknesses which can then be tackled in a systematic programme of remediation. A change of format would make it possible to record on the one form similar details for a group or whole class as in the class checklist of oral reading faults below.

Positive records use lists of reading skills the attainment of which are regarded as desirable at certain levels and for different purposes. Weakness noted in any skill listed indicates to you the need to work with the child in that precise area until satisfactory standards have been achieved. Such checklists are particularly

CLASS CHECKLIST	ORAL READING FAULTS													
Class .... Teacher														
Pupils	Word by word	Omission	Substitution	Addition	Reversal	Eye wandering	Guessing	Repetition	Poor phrasing	Poor punctuation	Weak phonic analysis	Weak syllabification	Finger pointing	Comments

helpful in that, not only do they give you a record of skills which pupils have actually acquired, they also remind you constantly of the need to diversify your teaching in order to encompass a wide range of reading skills. In order to judge how well or badly a pupil is faring in the acquisition of certain skills there has to be some criterion against which performance can be measured. Suppose a school thought it important to develop the skills listed below in the higher order skills checklist. In order to evaluate progress the staff would probably have to judge performance on the reading of certain texts which by experience they would agree to be of suitable standard at different reading levels. Such texts would not only need to be measured for readability but would also need to contain sufficient width and depth of treatment to make possible the sampling of the range of skills being reviewed. To record results and evaluate progress the school might find it necessary to devise individual record cards on the following lines:

HIGHER ORDER READING SKILLS CHECKLIST

Name ....

Date of birth ....

Class ....

Teacher ....

Skills	Comments
Gets main idea	
Recalls supporting details	
Makes inferences	
Draws conclusions	
Reads critically	
Skims for information	
Notes sequences	
Surveys new material	
Uses the context	
Appreciates mood/atmosphere	

Interpreting reading skill checklists

It is important that the information obtained by recording is interpreted insightfully and then applied in order to further the pupils' reading progress. For example, records reveal that a certain pupil tends to guess rather than identify words accurately. This could show up in the 'substitution' column in the oral reading faults checklist. What is important is not merely noting the fact of substitution but your ability to make inferences about the quality of the words substituted. For 'mother' – in the sentence, 'He bought a present for his mother' – a boy substitutes the word 'mummy'. This is a much more acceptable alternative than, say, 'moth'. It shows that the child is using the context and reading for meaning and that, in his case, substitutions are semantically correct and not therefore a cause for concern. On the other hand, the child who reads 'moth' for 'mother' appears to be deficient in a number of skills which merit detailed attention if reading for meaning is to be achieved.

It is important also to attempt to ascertain whether deficiencies in your own teaching are contributing to apparent weaknesses in your pupils. For example, from an appraisal of the higher order skills checklist above, a child is noted as being able to get the main idea and to recognise and recall the supporting details. However, he does not seem capable of comprehending at levels beyond the merely literal. Could it be that your own teaching practices have been limited to that area, that the child has the ability, but that you have not developed it?

Interest inventories and questionnaires

In the section 'The reluctant reader' I suggested how reading inventories, compiled by the children themselves, discussed periodically with you at individual reading interviews could be one way of encouraging them to read more.

There are, of course, many other ways in which the resulting data may be put to use. If the inventories were available to staff in general from time to time they could be used to extrapolate information on general trends and interests. This would be of concern to staff responsible for organising displays and exhibitions, for teachers planning visits and projects and for librarians and others responsible for ordering and organising books and other learning resources.

It is possible that for such purposes the pupil's own reading inventory lacks the kind of orderly arrangement which facilitates the extrapolation of information. If this is so, you might find that a structured questionnaire completed by the pupils themselves could provide you with the information you seek with greater precision and economy, as in the reading interests questionnaire below. Note that the format of the questionnaire on page 81 encourages the use of short answers so that the task of completing it does not become too much of a chore.

Children's interests are notoriously ephemeral. However, if the reading interests of an entire year group were investigated on completion of this type of questionnaire, certain broad trends would be discernible which teachers and librarians could then put to good use.

One obvious use is in guiding a child in his choice of books. For example, a child selects a book on his favourite hobby. You know the book is, for him, at frustration level so you suggest another on the same topic which he can read independently. When children show no interest in books it is often helpful to be aware of some outside interest or out-of-school activity on which they are really keen and to which reading can make a contribution. The classic case of such motivation is that recorded in Barry Hines's *A kestrel for a knave*, now renamed *Kes* after the film of that name.

```
┌─────────────────────────────────────────────────────────────────────┐
│  READING INTEREST QUESTIONNAIRE                                        │
├─────────────────────────────────────────────────────────────────────┤
│  Name .........................                                        │
├─────────────────────────────────────────────────────────────────────┤
```

1 Name your favourite comic

2 Name your favourite magazine

3 Name your favourite TV programme

4 Name your favourite radio programme

5 Who is your favourite author?

6 What is your favourite fiction book?

7 What is your favourite non-fiction book?

8 Which is your favourite newspaper?

9 Which parts of the newspaper do you like best? Put a tick in one of the
   spaces below

   Cartoons _____ Sport _____ News _____ Editorials _____ Woman's page _____

10 Which is your favourite film?

11 What is your favourite sport?

12 What hobbies do you have?

13 Which book has helped you most to enjoy your hobby?

14 Which book has helped you most at sport?

15 Name a book you would like the librarian to order

Pupils' own reading records

The records which pupils compile themselves of their own work probably have greater motivational value than records kept by teachers. They are especially valuable when they enable students to evaluate progress and to acquire realistic knowledge of their own strengths and weaknesses. In these respects the *SRA reading laboratories* are excellent. There is a permanent record of all work done in the student's workbook. There is a record of every error and of every correction. Progress is constantly recorded in comprehension, vocabulary development and spelling and also recorded is the time taken to complete each assignment. The reader is enabled to see at a glance improvement (or the lack of it) in the quality of his work and also his speed of working. When working with children at laboratory work I have been amazed at their capacity to use the recorded data for intelligent self-appraisal. For example, I have suggested to children who have scored at the 90 per cent level in four consecutive assignments that such a performance warrants promotion to the next colour band. Some, in reply, have pointed out that they would prefer to remain at a given level until they are scoring 100 per cent on two consecutive cards. Others have agreed that the comprehension and vocabulary work was of a high standard but that the work could have been done faster. They have then determined to effect significant improvements in both reading rate and speed of working before suggesting promotion. When asked how such improvements could be made their replies were quite realistic: e.g. they would concentrate on the work and not look round, they would make short notes and summaries in writing rather than trying to keep facts in their heads, they would survey only the important areas rather than read the whole text, or read the directions more thoroughly.

The designers of the *SRA reading laboratories* do not leave self-appraisal to chance. At the end of each assignment completed in the student's record book there is an exercise in evaluation. Readers are asked to rate the assignment in evaluate their own performance as being poor, fair, good or excellent. Most important, they are asked how they might improve their work on the next assignment by applying newly learned skills or adopting more effective strategies which they are encouraged to specify.

Unstructured pupil records

A good deal of information about children as readers can come to light if children are en-couraged to write reports or reviews of their recent reading. These are particularly valuable if the children can be critical about the quality or relevance of the content or style. Such reviews can form the basis for interesting discussions within groups and classes. Children are frequently stimulated to widen the range of their reading interests by hearing how other children have enjoyed certain books. Without such discussion about the quality and interest value of books which have been actually read many children would not acquire critical faculties or a sense of standards to apply when selecting books. We too can learn much from such activity about the criteria which adolescents apply to reading matter. By taking their views and preferences into account we can be realistic in the books we select for them or recommend to them.

Recording and the reading curriculum

So far I have looked at the question of record keeping mainly from the viewpoint of assessing individual progress in reading. However, the chief value of good records is in what they reveal about the quality of our teaching. Records should indicate to us how relevant are the goals we set, how adequate our plans for achieving them and the methods by which the plans are put into effect. If our records reveal to us that the reading needs of the children are not being met satisfactorily they indicate to us the need for a complete reappraisal of the reading curriculum we have devised. Some of the things we may need to reconsider are the following.

Physical conditions

The Bullock report tells us that English is one of the most poorly endowed of the secondary school subjects. It rarely has specialist rooms or adequate provision for display or storage. If reading is to be taught well the seating arrangements need to be flexible enough to cater for both group and individual instruction. Reading materials need to be easily accessible and attractively displayed. We need bookcases, newspaper racks and magazine stands and sufficient materials to allow for frequently changed displays and exhibitions to stimulate new interests.

Evaluation procedures

If all the children are to make progress we must constantly scrutinise our methods of evaluation. Perhaps one member of staff, given suitable training, could be responsible for this important area and could advise other staff on the use and interpretation of tests, both diagnostic and attainment. There is great need too to improve our methods of continuous assessment and to revise and record our observations, both formal and informal, of children developing as readers.

Organisation

There needs to be continuing dialogue on ways in which reading can be improved throughout the school. We need to plan for teaching methods at individual, group and class levels to make most efficient use of time, staff and materials and to meet different reading needs. We must decide which reading skills can be most effectively taught in isolation and which can be better integrated with other subjects. If some of the teaching is incidental we must ensure that it is not merely superficial but is deliberately planned and evaluated. There needs to be a detailed reading syllabus in every school so that sequential development in primary, intermediate and higher order skills is ensured. There needs to be much material designed and made by teachers themselves to supplement commercial apparatus.

Interaction

Time must be found so that from time to time there can be conferences between the teacher and individual children, between reading teacher and subject teachers on such matters as choice, readability and use of textbooks, between teacher and parents, between teacher and the schools psychological service for those with severe problems, and between teacher, child and librarian.

The need for reading specialists

At the moment the only people with expertise in teaching reading in middle and secondary schools are usually the staffs of remedial departments. Their main concern is with the teaching of primary skills with slow learners and underachievers. If reading is to be seen as a developmental process extending well into adulthood we need to concentrate much more on the extension skills with the majority of our children rather than on remedial work with just a few. We have been handicapped in the past by shortage of suitably trained staff capable of teaching and organising reading at many levels. LEA advisory services have suffered from similar shortages. However, in the last few years a number of colleges of education and universities have offered diploma and graduate courses in the teaching of reading at in-service level. A cadre of experts is growing. In addition many thousands of teachers have taken the two related courses of the Open University, *Reading development* and *Language and learning*, over the last few years. There is a great deal of latent expertise here. Shortly, these two courses with the addition of two practical modules will lead to the Diploma in Reading Development of the Open University. Soon then the dream of the Bullock report of a reading specialist in every school to coordinate every aspect of reading development could become a reality. In the meantime we must make the most of what we have. Schools must take into account the many practical difficulties when designing reading policies. Improvement will only come about by setting them and their staffs realistic targets at which to aim and by organising to achieve them steadily and systematically.

Part 3   A school language policy

by John Harris, Senior Lecturer in English,
Sheffield City Polytechnic

What is a language policy across the curriculum?

'For language to play its full role *as a means of learning*, the teacher must create in the classroom an environment which encourages a wide range of language uses.'
Language for life, 1975.12.3.

This sentence from the Bullock report puts in a nutshell the scope of a language policy – that it involves all teachers whatever their subject and that a concern with language stems from an awareness that it is one of the most crucial factors in successful learning.

The relationship between language and learning is summarised by the report in these terms:

'In the committee's view there are certain important inferences to be drawn from a study of the relationship between language and learning:
1 all genuine learning involves discovery, and it is ridiculous to suppose that teaching begins and ends with instruction as it is to suppose that "learning by discovery" means leaving children to their own resources;
2 language has a heuristic function: that is to say a child can learn by talking and writing as certainly as he can by listening and reading;
3 to exploit the process of discovery through language in all its uses is the surest means of enabling a child to master his mother tongue.'
Language for life, 1975.4.10.

A language policy involves an awareness about language and learning both for the individual teacher in relation to a specific subject area and for the whole staff of a school irrespective of subject specialisms. Language awareness involves, additionally, an understanding of how language works to mediate learning in all four of the language activities, talking, writing, listening and reading.

This section places the concern of the rest of the book with developing effective reading abilities into a wider context. It makes no sense in terms of educational and personal development to produce an efficient reader who is none the less deficient in the productive skills of talking and writing. Equally, for one teacher or one subject department to be working towards a language policy of the sort suggested in the Bullock report will be of limited value compared with a wider movement of most or all the staff being involved in such a venture.

All schools have a language policy in some sense, though many would not recognise that this was so. In the sense that we all make assumptions about the relationship between language and learning so schools have a language policy. But just as most individuals are unaware of the assumptions they make about language, so it is with schools. Essentially 'a language policy across the curriculum' is a process of recognising the assumptions, challenging them and moving towards a consensus of activities linked to a theoretical basis that is sound linguistically and educationally. It is a difficult, complex task and, in the second part of this section, we shall consider practical steps that can be taken. First, however, we must look at the issues in terms of reading, talking, listening and writing in more detail.

Can you identify any of your assumptions about language and learning? e.g. What do you think of a person who says, 'I come from 'Uddersfield'? What is your reaction to this piece of transcribed talk?
'...well, I er ... I'm not actually very certain about ... mm ... about (pause) what I mean is that his is a real prob, problem ...'

Try to work out the assumptions about language

in your school. You could get a colleague to do the same and compare notes.

What do you understand by the term 'curriculum'? Consider this quotation from a recent study by Douglas Barnes –

'What I mean by "curriculum" is the shaping of understanding, beliefs and values which goes on under the aegis of a school.'

Reading

There is a growing realisation that reading is not just the concern of the primary schools, nor, within middle and secondary schools, is it the concern only of the English or remedial specialists. At the same time the understanding is growing that after a child has *learned to read* he needs to be helped to *read to learn*. Nevertheless in many secondary schools the majority of staff do not regard any aspect of reading as their problem. As a consequence few children are given any positive teaching of higher reading skills or of related study skills. What the individual teacher can do is dealt with at length in the previous section. Here, and necessarily briefly, we shall look at four specific areas in which the whole staff, ideally, can collaborate in looking at reading across the curriculum.

Screening Identifying new intake pupils in need of particular help

In any intake into a comprehensive school there will inevitably be a number of children in urgent need of special help in reading. The number will vary according to locality and other factors. The school needs to identify these pupils quickly once they have settled in. To administer individual diagnostic tests would be a lengthy, expensive and, often, unnecessary procedure. All that is required initially is a simple test that is easy to administer and short in duration. Word reading

tests or a group test like GAP serve the purpose perfectly adequately, though these will not provide the detailed diagnostic information that is needed at a later stage for those pupils identified as being in need of extra help. For further information about the range of tests see page 32.

Once information has been gathered, it needs to be disseminated to all the staff involved. This should be the responsibility of a language policy coordinator, a point that is developed later.

Coordination with remedial teachers

Many secondary schools have remedial teachers who have had specialist training, or who have, for whatever reason, devoted themselves to working with the slow learner. If a language policy is to be effective across the range of subjects close liaison needs to be established and maintained between remedial and subject teachers. In my experience remedial units can all too easily become isolated from the mainstream of activities and the valuable widening of perspectives that arises from an interchange of knowledge about pupils and discussion of approaches is lost. Again a coherent policy is needed. Pupils who are 'released' from the secure and supportive remedial unit into the outside world of the school may, in fact, become reading 'recidivists' if there is no contact between the two groups of teachers. Where a policy of withdrawal groups for language and reading development exists there needs to be an involvement of all staff responsible for teaching the children concerned.

Textbooks and worksheets

Teachers are frequently placed in the position of having to use textbooks with which they are not happy because more suitable ones either have not been written or are too expensive to purchase. For a school to be able to institute a policy of control over textbooks so that choice can be made in terms of readability and motivational levels would be fortunate – but largely unrealistic. We have to live with what we have got, these days. However, there is no doubt that a major source of frustration and inefficient learning is the use of textbooks that are not suited to the reading abilities of the pupils. One might add, as a secondary point, the absence of help in how to use textbooks either in whole or in part.

It would be possible, but not desirable in view of the time and effort involved, for a school to look at the readability levels of all textbooks and coursebooks in use in the school, though the procedure can be adopted for sets of new books being considered for purchase. More practically, teachers who have built up an awareness of the language capabilities of a particular group of children are able with reasonable reliability to pick out areas of particular difficulty in textbooks not of their own subject area. Points to look for include terminology that causes confusion such as unexplained technical language and sections where a combination of reading difficulty and content of low intrinsic interest can effect total non-comprehension.

Much more can be done by teachers to provide assistance through positive teaching. Providing children with a scheme of what they are expected to find within a particular reading assignment will help them overcome many reading hurdles.

Worksheets have become popular as a result of dissatisfaction with coursebooks and textbooks. And, in so far as the language used is under the control of the teacher who knows the children using the materials, this is a step forward. The possibility of monitoring the level of reading difficulty exists. Several recent research projects, however, have shown that an apparent failure to solve problems in Maths, for example,

or to assimilate knowledge in other subject areas arises, in fact, from the child's inability to cope with the reading level of the instructions and exposition on the worksheet or workcard or in the textbook. A useful project is to scrutinise the language of such materials. Ask a colleague from a different subject area to look at the materials considering these questions –

Is the language used likely to cause a reading problem?

Are the instructions too complex?

Is the task adequately described?

If there is any doubt, use a simple word deletion exercise with a small sample of children to check. Delete every tenth word from the text of a worksheet and ask the children to supply the missing words. A percentage of 50–60 correct answers is generally regarded as satisfactory. Ideally the test should be at least 300 words in length.

Topic work and libraries

More and more teachers are using a topic approach in the lower secondary years either influenced by primary practice or under the constraint of interdisciplinary work. Whatever the merits of this approach, there are implications for a language policy. Experience in junior schools has shown that if topic work is not carefully controlled children are likely to engage in reading tasks well beyond their capabilities and, as a result, produce ill-digested or even directly copied written versions of what they have found in reference books. Children often abandon such work under a weight of frustration. Clearly no useful educational purpose is being served.

Close liaison between the teachers planning the work and library staff is essential. Library staff need to be able not merely to point children to relevant books, but to books and other materials that will present to the pupil *a realisable reading task*. This is the necessary foundation for any genuine learning through topic work.

At appropriate times the school should ensure that children are taught the basic skills of using a library and how to find their way around simple reference books.

Talking

We talk for many purposes. In the context of school there are two main forms of talk, *expository* and *exploratory*. Other forms of talk are obviously to be found, but these two dominate and suggest two distinct attitudes to pupil-learning. The contrast is often made between the child-centred approach of many primary schools and the subject-centred approach at the secondary phase. Clearly such a distinction is crude and distorts the complex range of attitudes and practice to be found in both phases of education. Yet there remains when all qualifications have been made some element of truth in the contrast. The charac-teristic picture of the primary classroom is of children collaborating with the teacher and each other in learning, grouped round tables to facilitate this activity. This is the setting for exploratory talk. The setting for expository talk is the serried rows of desks still characteristic of many secondary classrooms – an image that is analogous with the lecture-room and one suggestive of the exposition of a body of knowledge transmitted to passive learners.

What sorts of talk are facilitated by the layout of furniture in your classroom?

Why should the difference outlined in the last paragraph be a cause for concern? Fundamen-tally it is because a recognition of the part that talking plays in successful learning suggests that the use solely of the expository form of talk – teacher lecturing to the class – cuts many children off from the intellectual growth that as teachers we are trying to help the children achieve. It is through exploratory talk that children reach towards their own formulations of concepts and ideas and come to see the inter-relatedness of bits of knowledge.

The top transcript opposite records a group of children engaged in exploratory talk, striving towards sorting out a range of technical terms. Have they learned anything? It is not easy to make a positive answer. At least we can say that the children, despite the felt presence of the teacher ('he'), are able to formulate their own questions as a necessary beginning of the process of answering them. Through exploration we come to construct hypotheses and by testing these in a secure context we develop the confidence to make them public. All too often the nature of pupil–teacher dialogue demands the final public stage without either of the two preliminaries. In-adequate and incomplete learning or frustration are the result.

Not all talk in a lesson will be exploratory, of course. There is a legitimate area for expository talk and for the dialogue between pupil and teacher. Most dialogue between teacher and child consists of the teacher questioning the child. What happens? The bottom transcript shows a typical exchange. The teacher asks what appears to be an open question, but, from his rejection, however tactful, of the pupils' answers it is obvious that he has in mind a 'right' answer and that he will accept no other. It is an unconscious classroom quiz game. Does it help the children learn effectively? A detailed sequence of activities for looking at teacher–pupil interaction is suggested later in this section.

88

IST GIRL:	I think the lochs are interesting.
BOY:	Let's see how many there are. All them sea-areas, he called them lochs –
IST GIRL:	Sea-lochs.
IST GIRL:	It's funny though. This side is very different. It goes up in fjords.
BOY:	They're not fjords – lochs.
IST GIRL:	These inlets here are fjords.
BOY:	Ay, but he called them lochs.
IST GIRL:	It's just them little bits here.
2ND GIRL:	Little bits of rock. They're fjords.
BOY:	It's not.
IST GIRL:	Were you here yesterday? Is this all about Scotland? (referring to atlas)
BOY:	Loch Ness and all these little lochs. Loch Mare.
IST GIRL:	Loch Roddy.
BOY:	Loch Ull.
IST GIRL:	I know they're all lochs you can't have fjords like these little ones going in.
BOY:	That's the geographical name for it, isn't it? They call them lochs. They still call them lochs.
IST GIRL:	I know, but they're still fjords, aren't they? I mean, land, when it goes on like that, you call it fjords but all water you call lochs.
BOY:	If there's a river coming off it, I just call it a firth.
IST GIRL:	They're river estuaries, aren't they, them firths? So all the ones that that have got no rivers, I call them lochs.

TEACHER:	Looking at the photograph, what is the first thing that strikes you? Looking at it first of all?
PUPIL:	Sir, the picture was taken from far away.
TEACHER:	Ye-e-s. Anything else? About the farm itself? Yes?
PUPIL:	It's in a valley.
TEACHER:	It's in a valley, yes. Yes?
PUPIL:	(inaudible)
TEACHER:	Yes? Anything else? The thing that struck me looking at this – (pupil interrupts)
PUPIL:	It's a small farm.
TEACHER:	It's a small farm – and something else about it?
PUPIL:	There's a lot of stone around. (various other inaudible replies, none accepted)
PUPIL:	It's deserted.
TEACHER:	Well, I wouldn't say that. We're obviously going to study the farm if someone lives on the farm.
PUPIL:	It's isolated.
TEACHER:	Good lad. It's an *isolated* farm. It's a good word. This is the first thing that struck me looking at this, how isolated the farm is . . . so that's a good word. The farms in Iceland are *isolated*.

Listening

Listening occupies children for as much as half their time in the classroom, yet it is the least thought about of the language activities. Even the Bullock report devotes no more than one and a half pages out of 600 to the topic. Research on listening would hardly fill a briefcase whereas research on reading would fill many pantechnicons. Two general points can be made:

● Ability in listening appropriately in different situations seems to be taken for granted, yet there is reason to suppose that the particular listening skills involved in any language situation are not naturally present but require active and systematic development as do the skills of speaking, writing and reading.

● Such evidence of listening comprehension as is available suggests that many children at secondary level operate at a very low level in their listening.

Some ways of assisting the child to listen more effectively.

The listener should:
(a) face the speaker so that eye contact can be established and gesture be received;
(b) not be speaking or writing or in any other way distracted while listening.

The speaker should:
(a) use movement, gesture, eye movement and physical stance in such a way as to support, not detract from, the message;
(b) vary voice appropriately;
(c) not overestimate the concentration span of the listeners;
(d) provide supporting visual materials to vary the object of attention from time to time, while making clear to the audience what it is they should, at any given time, be attending to;
(d) sequence the material for exposition logically, preferably providing a digest at the beginning to help the listener know where he is;
(e) suit the use of language to the listener rather than the subject and to the listeners' powers of abstraction and reasoning.

Writing

It is a truism that whereas the primary teacher can see all of a child's writing in a given span of time, the secondary teacher will see but a small percentage. There are children who write successfully in one subject area but not in others and children who achieve little success in any. To help with difficulties every teacher concerned with a particular child's education needs to be aware of the whole picture. Concerted rather than fragmented help is necessary.

An increasing number of teachers are becoming aware that attention to writing is not the sole preserve of the English specialist but of all teachers. To be working towards an effective language policy across the curriculum means involving teachers from different subject areas looking at the range, quality and types of writing expected of a child.

Three questions to ask about your children's writing:

What purpose does it serve?
What forms do they use?
Who do they write to?

The purpose of writing

Writing, like talking, has a learning function as well as giving the teacher evidence of what has been learned. Douglas Barnes makes the distinction in terms of *transmission* and *interpretation* of knowledge. We are all aware of writing that tells us how many facts have been remembered, for example. That is writing to transmit knowledge. Writing for the interpretation of knowledge is less obvious.

If you listen to a conversation it is often apparent that people talk to come, perhaps unconsciously, to a realisation of what it is they actually think and also to make sense of a particular experience or phenomenon. This is why when something exciting has happened we feel a need to talk about it. This same language function can be achieved in a solitary way through writing – not writing as it is usually understood in terms of the school essay or factual record, but the writing that precedes public presentation, the jottings and personal notes, the sometimes almost incoherent, because unshaped, formulations that are made, as it were, to oneself. As in talk, there is a sequence that makes for effective learning.

Writing for interpretation is often given the technical name 'expressive' writing – writing for trying out ideas and for coming to terms with new experiences – and this type is crucial to the early stages of any learning of new concepts or evaluating new experiences. Adult modes of writing, termed 'transactional', are what the child is expected to employ in most of his writing at secondary stage, apart from stories, plays and poems which are given the label of 'poetic' writing. Recent research has shown (Martin et al., 1976) that 'expressive function' writing accounts for a mere 6 per cent of school writing in the first years of the secondary school. For a child who is failing to achieve success in writing, it may be that the predominant mode of writing expected by the school is the main obstacle to success.

Variety of forms

Hand in hand with our concern to see the purpose of a piece of writing we should look also at the actual forms of writing expected of a child. The traditional divisions between factual and non-factual, personal and impersonal are neither particularly useful in themselves nor are

AUDIENCE BY YEAR
(percentages of year sample)

	Yr 1	Yr 3	Yr 5	Yr 7
Self	0	0	0	0
Trusted adult	2	3	2	1
Pupil-teacher dialogue	51	45	36	19
Teacher examiner	40	45	52	61
Peer group	0	0	0	0
Public	0	1	5	6
Miscellaneous (translation dictation, exercises etc.)	7	6	5	13

AUDIENCE BY SUBJECT
(percentages of subject sample)

	Eng	Hist	Geog	RE	Sci
Self*	0	0	0	0	0
Trusted adult	5	0	0	4	0
Pupil-teacher dialogue	65	17	13	64	7
Teacher examiner	18	69	81	22	87
Peer group	0	0	0	0	0
Public	6	0	0	0	0
Miscellaneous	6	14	6	10	6

* The research team considered that in any involved writing the self was a significant part of the writer's sense of audience. They therefore defined the category for their purposes as covering items obviously unconnected with an audience – rough work for instance.

FUNCTION BY YEAR

	Yr 1	Yr 3	Yr 5	Yr 7
Transactional	54	57	62	84
Expressive	6	6	5	4
Poetic	17	23	24	7
Miscellaneous	23	14	9	5

FUNCTION BY SUBJECT

	Eng	Hist	Geog	RE	Sci
Transactional	34	88	88	57	92
Expressive	11	0	0	11	0
Poetic	39	2	0	12	0
Miscellaneous	26	10	12	20	8

they necessarily instructive in the school context. Anyone familiar with the writing of primary school children knows that at that stage no child is more than reaching tentatively towards the sorts of writing in a subject area that as adults we tend to take for granted. To expect the child who is only a summer holiday away from junior school to cope with the demand to write 'scientifically', 'geographically' or 'historically' is, of course, to ask the impossible of most children.

A school should, therefore, be looking at the variety of forms that a child is allowed to use; should be observing in which particular forms a child can achieve success and progress on his own terms; should, then, endeavour to relate these forms of writing to the expectations of acquiring knowledge in a subject area.

Some forms to think about using:
personal record – i.e. the child determines not only the content of what he writes, but also the form in which he organises it.

commentary – again the form and selection of content is a matter of personal choice. The teacher is, of course, free to initiate a dialogue with the child if he feels the selection is inadequate.

reports – this form of writing can be carefully controlled in terms of the form and the audience, and, in most subject areas, provides a productive bridge from the undifferentiated writing of the primary years to the 'adult' models expected at the upper secondary stage.

stories – these need not be just in English or 'creative writing'!

lists of questions formulated by the child with suggested answers – the importance of this is, surely, that identifying what you wish to know and trying to establish what you do know is the basis of learning. Such writing allows the child 'take stock' and plan further stages of learning for himself with, again, the necessary collaboration of the teacher.

Audience

The third dimension of writing under scrutiny is how the writer sees his reader. The image the writer holds in mind of his reader is a major constraint on how the writing is done. We might, for example, write to a trusted friend quite freely recounting an unhappy experience, but to write about the same experience to someone we know hardly at all would be much more difficult. A research project at the London Institute of Education has looked at the sense of audience in children's writing and the research team suggests the following categories:

1 Child to self (diaries, private notes, first draft writing).
2 Child to trusted adult (sympathetic response expected).
3 Pupil to teacher as partner in dialogue.
4 Pupil to teacher seen as examiner or assessor.
5 Child to his peers.
6 Writer to his reader (an unknown audience).

The significant findings are that throughout the secondary school categories 3 and 4 dominate and that as a child progresses up the age-range category 3 becomes less and less significant (see table on page 91). The inference is plainly that, as the child sees it, the majority of his school writing is for the teacher as examiner, concerns the transmission of knowledge – or ignorance? – and has little or nothing to do with the mental, emotional or social development of the writer.

Other questions to consider about your pupils' writing:

Can you see evidence of learning as a result of a piece of writing?

How much of the writing is directly copied from source material? What does this imply?

How do you respond to a piece of writing? Would you be happy to receive the comments that you put on someone's work? How would you feel if there were no comment? In your comments have you been encouraging, constructive, damning or simply indifferent?

Did the writing you set present the child with a realistically achievable task?

How much freedom and initiative did the task allow the child?

Implementation of a language policy

We have, then, looked in general at the idea of a language policy across the curriculum and at each of the four areas of language activity in more detail. We will now consider the strategies and problems of implementation.

Every school has its own particular structure and character and means of implementing any new policy in a school will vary. There is no blueprint for implementing a language policy. The small middle school with a staff of less than twenty presents an entirely different organisational problem to the comprehenseive school with a staff of nearly a hundred. What will work for one will not necessarily work for the other. In a small school all staff can easily be involved in decision taking and communication at a personal level is possible. There is more likely to be a set of assumptions held in common about teaching styles, about modes of contact between staff and pupils, and this provides a growth point for specific attention to the question of language and learning. Many middle schools already possess on the staff someone with responsibility for English and language work. Initiatives can quite naturally be taken by that member of staff, backed by the Head, without other members of staff feeling put-upon. The fact that middle schools recruit staff who are primary trained means that these teachers see

themselves, by and large, as general teachers and an interest in language and learning across the curriculum areas is correspondingly easier to promote than in the secondary school.

Who to involve initially?

Where there is existing machinery within a school for the implementation of new policies, there is no need to establish anything new for a language policy. If, however, there is no machinery, experience in those schools that have initiated a policy suggests that working on a small scale and informally with a nucleus of staff who may well be drawn together by some interest shared is most likely to create success.

For instance, if a group of teachers are involved in a programme of Integrated Studies ranging across traditional curriculum boundaries they will provide a natural spearhead for implementing a language policy, taking realisable starting points such as looking at the range of writing expected in the programme with a class or at the reading levels of textbooks and other materials used in the teaching. A report back to a staff meeting, or staff seminar, would be a logical step towards increasing the number of staff interested. It is important to stress that a language policy cannot be imposed. It must grow and grow gradually. The growth must not be haphazard and it will be the job of the coordinator to think ahead and anticipate second and third stages if these do not naturally suggest themselves. A one-off activity will lead to an upsurge of interest which will fade away if successive steps are not planned.

Whose is the responsibility?

There is no question about ultimate responsibility for introducing and supporting a language policy. It must rest with the Head. Normally the Head will need to delegate executive responsibility to a senior member of staff who is qualified or sufficiently interested to gain expertise in the language area. Unless a senior member is chosen the process of working towards a policy will lack credibility and prestige. Many schools have a Director of Studies. Such a person is ideally placed in organisational terms, to oversee the implementation of a language policy.

What about the head of English?

The head of the English department ought to be closely involved in the work and may well become a key advisory person, but it is probably unwise for him to carry the main executive responsibility. This might lead to the policy being seen as the concern only of the English department or as a bid for extending the influence of the department within the school. A language policy must be seen as a school matter and as involving all the staff on equal terms.

Is documentation necessary?

We live in an age of circulars and memoranda. There is an understandable inclination to initiate a policy by the publication of a document giving a blueprint for the school. With the constraints of a wider public audience in mind – LEA Advisers, Education Officers to name but two – some schools have begun in this way. Several dangers exist in such a beginning. To publish a blueprint suggests that a language policy is finite; a language policy, however, is a matter of process and to suggest the end-point in an initial statement will prejudge issues and may preclude valuable lines of development later. Publishing a document does not necessarily bring about action; it may well be regarded as a substitute and the language policy will be filed away indefinitely. Staff should be enabled to see the language policy as something that concerns them and the children they teach, not as a reaction to outside pressures or fashions in education.

In a limited way, and couched in suitable terms, publishing a document within the school may serve some purpose. Such a document should do no more than open up issues and suggest starting points. It might, for instance, contain relevant extracts from the Bullock report with suggestions for action in one area. It must be remembered that working towards a language policy forces teachers to question eventually their own uses of language at a personal and professional level. None of us takes that kindly. Tact, therefore, is crucial. An initial document is to be seen as opening up questions, not as a directive that, by unwittingly posing a threat, will prove counter-productive.

The role of the coordinator

We can make some general points about the role of the coordinator based on the experiences of some schools that have initiated a language policy.

● He will need to be identified with the Head in the first initiatives.

● He will need to find from among the staff those who are most likely to form a nucleus for action. It might be, as previously suggested, a group of staff engaged in team-teaching, or a group associated with the teaching of a year group.

● He will provide information for all staff relating to what is going on in the school in the language area.

● At a later stage he will need to be the 'publisher' of reports from working parties and to provide supporting information such as theoretical readings relating to work in progress.

● He should personally be engaged in an area of investigation and maintain a contact with all projects that are going on, offering help, if needed, and encouragement.

• He should have time available for talking to all members of staff, not just those already engaged in an aspect of the work.

• He will be responsible for bringing in 'expert' assistance and, of course, for making the difficult decision as to if and when such help is likely to prove useful.

• He might try to establish informal links, either directly or through the local Teachers' Centre, with neighbouring schools engaged in similar work.

Sequencing the development of a language policy

Although it has been stated that there cannot be a blueprint for a language policy applicable to every school, some lines of development can be suggested. These will need to be adapted sympathetically to local conditions. We look first at writing and reading and follow this with a section on the problematic area of teacher–pupil interaction in the context of classroom discourse.

Writing - a sequence of investigation

No policy for developing more effective learning through attention to the way language is used can start without knowledge of what is actually happening. In the area of writing the business of collecting information is comparatively easy. There needs, however, to be some framework within which the collecting can be done, as well as the subsequent analysis.

A possible starting point is to collect all the writing done by a child in one week to clarify what demands are being made across the curriculum. Concern has been widely expressed about the amount of ill-defined and even unnecessary written work that children are asked to do at secondary level. Areas of interest that might lead to fruitful action will be opened up if a working party look at collected samples asking the simple question 'Why was this work set?'

A second stage should involve a wider range of samples, work over a longer period of time collected from a range of children of different abilities. The work should be looked at in terms of what sort of task has been asked of the children, using a simple classification system such as this:

• Direct copying – from textbook, blackboard or at dictation.

• Note making in which the child's own summary skills are exercised.

• Limited answer writing such as tests of factual knowledge or spelling tests.

• Recording based on observation.

• Writing that requires the ordering of facts – one purpose of essay work.

• Writing that calls for interpretation of fact.

• Writing that allows for the expression of personal attitudes and opinions.

No classification system should be taken for granted. Discussion of the validity of a classification system will open up fundamental questions about the function of writing in the process of learning.

Five further stages:

• Looking at samples of writing in terms of audience.

• Seeing how far written work set relates to the distinction made earlier between writing for interpretation and writing for transmission.

• Asking how far in the reception and further use of writing is it apparent that staff are regarding the work as an instrument for positive teaching.

● Looking at how written work is corrected. What, for example, is done by different teachers about spelling? Can there be a coordinated policy by which spelling problems are anticipated instead of the fatalistic attitudes so prevalent that all work related to spelling is 'remedial' in its fundamental sense?

● Attempting to evaluate the gradation of difficulty of writing tasks confronting a child as he progresses through the school.

Covering these topics in depth would engage a working party in a long series of discussions, even after the work samples had been sorted out. Clearly not everything can be done at once. Progress must be gradual. Those serving on working parties will, after all, be teaching!

Links with reading

Some of the areas of investigation suggested in the writing sequence lead naturally into reading activities. The question of subject-specific vocabulary is as much a reading problem as a writing problem. Copying also. If a child is copying to any great extent he will not be learning anything of educational value. Is it a reading problem or a writing problem? Copying may occur when the reader is beyond frustration level. It may occur when he does not know why he is meant to be doing some writing, or when he sees the object of the writing as unnecessary. Ask yourselves these questions:

Is the reading assignment realistic?

Has the child understood the nature of the writing task?

If you investigate several cases of copying from these points of view not only will the inter-relatedness of language work be obvious, but positive teaching strategies will result.

Reading –
a sequence of investigation

Since the rest of this book is concerned with reading development and the individual teacher, we shall be content in this context to offer a limited range of activities that should impinge on a group of teachers or even the whole staff.

● Initially the passing on of information gathered from a screening exercise is necessary. If the school has a separate Remedial unit a specialist from the unit should discuss the implications of the test findings with all the staff teaching the first-year intake.

● If a number of children in a year group are withdrawn from their normal teaching group for special help in reading, their progress must be monitored and reported back to the teachers who have to integrate the children at a later stage back into the main teaching groups. The specialist teacher should be in a position to offer suggestions to the subject specialists and this might well be done through the language work coordinator who can be seen as a 'neutral' and embarrassment between colleagues avoided.

● Subject departments should consider the procedures adopted for introducing technical terminology in their own subject area and see how this relates to reading tasks. A useful exercise is for departments to come together to exchange their findings.

● A similar pooling of ideas for positive teaching strategies to prepare pupils for reading assign-ments (e.g. homework reading tasks – Is it adequate to say 'read chapter 3'? What structured help can be offered so that the pupils know in outline what they should be looking for while they are reading?).

● Analysis of the reading levels of worksheets, workcards, handouts and similar materials.

● The introduction of a study skills course for 'A' level pupils at the beginning of their sixth-form career to promote efficient reading of different types of texts and effective use of library resources.

Classroom interaction

The question of how staff talk to children and children to staff and to each other is the most difficult aspect of a language policy. It is not the best starting point because it can easily be seen as an intrusion into the private domain of the individual teacher. However, the problem has to be faced. The coordinator of the language policy should look for a small group of staff, even just two, who have sufficient mutual trust to enable them to investigate this area and report findings to a larger group of staff. These teachers will be in a very exposed position and should have the total support of the coordinator and Head. The handling of discussion at the report-back session will require care. If possible this work should engage members of at least two subject departments.

There are several ways of recording teacher–pupil interaction in the classroom. If possible video-taping of lessons provides the best format for subsequent analysis. If the equipment is not available in school it is worth while trying other local educational institutions – Teachers' Centres, a Polytechnic, a College of Education (if any are left). Audio tapes are a perfectly reasonable second best. Care is needed with selecting the type of microphone and placing it to obtain a fair recording. Failing any mechanical aid that will allow for a leisured recall of lessons, one member of staff can sit in on another's lesson and make notes for future discussion.

What to look for

There have been several schedules devised for looking at classroom interaction. A simple beginning is necessary. As a first stage it should suffice to break down the lesson time in terms of the actual amount of time the teacher spends talking, the time occupied by teacher–pupil dialogue and by pupil-to-pupil exchanges. Flanders (1970) asserts that from his observations of classroom interaction two-thirds of each lesson is taken up with talk and that two-thirds of that is done by the teacher. See page 98 for his analysis schedule.

How to progress

Once a start has been made, even by only a few members of staff, a more sophisticated analysis schedule can be employed. The most useful is that devised by Douglas Barnes (see page 99), which focusses attention on the nature of the teacher's questions, the pupil's participation, the language of instruction and the language of relationships. The use of such a schedule by pairs of teachers particularly if they are from different subject departments will provide illumination of language styles used in teaching and a powerful basis for developing uses of language that are most appropriate to effective learning.

Is theory necessary?

All that has been suggested and argued in this section has drawn upon a body of linguistic theory which for present purposes has had to remain largely implicit. As a school progresses along the road of implementing a language policy, questions wlll be raised that require answers of a theoretical nature. It is in this context that members of the English department ought to be able to offer special help to their colleagues. This, however, may not always be the case. The coordinator of the language policy will need to undertake back-up reading himself and provide a lead for the rest of the staff. In most localities support is available from LEA advisers, HMIs and wardens of teachers'

FLANDERS' INTERACTIVE ANALYSIS CATEGORIES* (FIAC)		
Teacher talk	Response	1 *Accepts feeling* Accepts and clarifies an attitude or the feeling tone of a pupil in a non-threatening manner. Feelings may be positive or negative. Predicting and recalling feelings are included. 2 *Praises or encourages* Praises or encourages pupil action or behaviour. Jokes that release tension, but not at the expense of another individual; nodding head, or saying 'Um hm?' or 'go on' are included. 3 *Accepts or uses ideas of pupils* Clarifying, building, or developing ideas suggested by a pupil. Teacher extensions of pupil ideas are included but as the teacher brings more of his own ideas into play, shift to category 5.
		4 *Asks questions* Asking a question about content or procedure, based on teacher ideas, with the intent that a pupil will answer.
	Initiation	5 *Lecturing* Giving facts or opinions about content or procedures; expressing *his own* ideas, giving *his own* explanation, or citing an authority other than a pupil.
		6 *Giving directions* Directions, commands, or orders to which a pupil is expected to comply.
		7 *Critising or justifying authority* Statements intended to change pupil behaviour from nonacceptable to acceptable pattern; bawling someone out; stating why the teacher is doing what he is doing; extreme self-reverence.
	Response	8 *Pupil talk – response* Talk by pupils in response to teacher. Teacher initiates the contact or solicits pupil statement or structures the situation. Freedom to express own ideas is limited.
Pupil talk	Initiation	9 *Pupil talk – initiation* Talk by pupils which they initiate. Expressing own ideas; initiating a new topic; freedom to develop opinions and a line of thought, like asking thoughtful questions; going beyond the existing structure.
	Silence	10 *Silence or confusion* Pauses, short periods of silence and periods of confusion in which communication cannot be understood by the observer.

* There is no scale implied by these numbers. Each number is classificatory; it designates a particular kind of communication event. To write these numbers down during observation is to enumerate not to judge a position on a scale.

centres. Where there is a local Polytechnic, College of Education or University Institute of education qualified and experienced staff will be at hand to offer consultation – school-based consultancy is a concept of in-service work, as yet in its infancy, but with exciting possibilities which it is to be hoped will develop over the next few years. The decision to bring in outside help is difficult and can only be taken in the light of the particular circumstances in a school. For the school unable or unwilling to draw on expert help guidance over which books are of most value is given in the final section of this book.

A footnote

Many teachers reading this section will be saying 'that's all very well, but not in our school'. They will be thinking of the attitudes of the Head and staff, concluding that the initiation of a language policy is a hopeless pipe-dream. As has been said before, a language policy across the curriculum makes us look at our own behaviour as teachers and talkers in a way that many will reject out of hand. In some schools, therefore, there will be teachers wanting to make a start of some sort, but recognising that they are very much by themselves receiving from their colleagues not

Below: analysis schedule devised by Douglas Barnes

(a) *Teacher's questions*
Analyse *all* questions asked by the teacher into these categories:
1   factual ('what?' questions)
      (i) meaning
      (ii) information
2   reasoning ('how?' and 'why?' questions)
      (i) 'closed' reasoning – recalled sequences
      (ii) 'closed' reasoning – not recalled
      (iii) obersavtions
3   'open' questions not calling for reasoning
4   Social
      (i) control ('won't you . . . ?' questions)
      (ii) appeal (aren't we . . . ?' questions)
      (iii) other

(b) *Pupil's participation*
1   Was all speech initiated by the teacher? Note any exchanges initiated by pupil.
      (i) If these were initiated by questions were they 'what?', 'how?' or 'why?' questions? Were they directed towards the material studied or towards performing the given tasks?
      (ii) If they were unsolicited statements or comments, how did the teacher deal with them?
2   Were pupils required to express personal responses
      (i) of perception?
      (ii) of feeling and attitude?
3   How large a part did pupils take in the lesson? Were any silent throughout? How large a proportion took a continuous part in the discussion?
4   What did pupils' contribution show of their success in following the lesson?
5   How did the teacher deal with inappropriate contributions?

(c) *The language of instruction*
1   Did the teacher use a linguistic register specific to his subject? Find examples of vocabulary and structure characteristic of the register?
2   Did any pupils attempt to use this register? Was it expected of them?
3   What did the teacher do to mediate between the language and experience of his pupils and the language and concepts of the subject?
4   Did the teacher use forms of language which, though not specific to his subject, might be outside the range of eleven-year-olds? Find examples, if any.

(d) *Social relationships*
1   How did the relationship between the teacher and pupils show itself in language?
2   Were the differences between the language of instruction and the language of relationships? Was the language of relationship intimate or formal? Did it vary during the lesson?

(e) *Language and other media*
1   Was language used for any tasks that might have been done better by other means (e.g. pictures, practical tasks, demonstrations)?
2   Were pupils expected to verbalize any non-verbal tasks they were engaged in?

just indifference but sometimes active hostility. Can they achieve anything?

The answer is unequivocally that even a few teachers can have an influence, albeit limited, and that some sort of beginning is better than none. Much that has been suggested in this section and in the previous section in terms of reading will help the individual teacher in his own subject area or, in the middle school, in his teaching programme.

Although a limited initiative will not bring about a radical growth of awareness throughout a school of language as a means of effecting genuine learning, in the sense that any child or group of children may be helped towards more effective learning the effort will have been worth while.

I am grateful to my colleague Tony Baldwin for permission to reproduce material on page 89.

See page 132 for References/bibliography.

Part 4   Resources

by John L. Foster, Lord Williams' School, Thame

What do children really read?

In spite of the fact that there are over 100 educational publishers producing books for secondary schools and that there has been a boom in the children's book market over the last fifteen years, a considerable number of teenagers leave school with a dismissive attitude towards books, reluctant to turn to them either for information or enjoyment. Surveys, such as that conducted by the Schools Council Research Project into the reading habits of children aged between ten and fifteen, have indicated that the percentage of children in a year group showing little interest in books increases between the ages of ten and fifteen. The range of books, both fiction and non-fiction, for ten- to sixteen-year-olds of all reading abilities, available in the classroom, in libraries and in bookshops continues to widen, yet the trend towards disinterest is still noticeable among certain secondary pupils.

What do you think are the reasons why the number of pupils who reject books increases between the ages of ten and sixteen?

Although there is a falling-off of interest in books in some pupils aged ten to sixteen, many of these non-book-readers continue to read both for information and enjoyment. Among the younger ones comics, as their sales figures show, remain popular. Older boys read either newspapers or magazines that cater for their specialised interests, for example, fishing, motorcycling, football or photography. Older girls read the magazines such as *Oh Boy!* and *Mates* that are specially produced for teenagers. Most of them are weekly, fairly inexpensive, and have circulations ranging from just over 100000 to over 500000 in the case of the most popular one, *Jackie*. There are also several monthly magazines like *Look Now* and *19*, which are more expensive

and which have circulations around 200000. Many of those teenagers who are non-book-readers read such magazines.

What comics, magazines and newspapers do the pupils in your classes read?

Only a few books are ever as widely read by teenagers as the magazines are. These are books that are related to a current film or television series. In the early 1970s, at the time of the film, Erich Segal's *Love story* was extremely popular, and in 1976 Peter Benchley's *Jaws* was avidly read by teenagers as well as adults. An interesting feature of the *Jaws* phenomenon was that the book was, in certain instances, read by pupils who otherwise rejected books completely or who displayed such a lack of stamina in any other reading situation that they surprised their teachers by their ability to cope with a novel of such length.

What paperback books related to a film or a television series are currently being read by pupils in your classes?

A number of conclusions can be drawn from the fact that comics and magazines and books tied in to films or television programmes provide the most popular reading among secondary school pupils. The most significant one for the teacher of reading is the implication that pupils who become non-book-readers may do so because they do not want to read the books that are being offered them, rather than because they do not want to read at all. What it is important to do, therefore, is to find books for such pupils that they will want to read as much as they want to read magazines or books in, for example, the *Bionic Man* series.

It is impossible to predict which particular book will appeal to an individual child. However, there is evidence from the Schools Council survey into children's reading habits that narrative books are more widely read than non-narrative books. There is evidence too from teachers working with reluctant readers that the fiction provided in such series as *Pyramids*, *Topliners* and *Getaway* is often the way in to the world of books for many young readers.

The popularity of the *Topliner* series cannot be denied, yet it is sometimes criticised on the grounds that many of the books are non-quality narratives. However, quality, though desirable, is not initially essential. Wide reading ultimately leads to discrimination. Teachers of reading in the ten to sixteen age range need to be alert to the danger of offering pupils books that are too demanding before they are ready for them. To succeed with the reluctant reader it is necessary to start with his own interests and the books that he is willing to choose to read. In that way you stand a chance of leading him on to the quality books that you would like him to be reading. If you aim too high at first you run the risk of turning him against books.

What are your views on making non-quality narrative books available in the classroom and in the school library?

Is it better for children to read anything rather than nothing? Do we worry too much about the 'rubbish'? Are there any books that you should actively discourage children from reading?

A school book-buying policy

Since narrative plays so important a part in developing the enjoyment of reading among middle and secondary school pupils, it is important that an adequate supply of fiction should be made available for class use, in classroom libraries and in the school library. Ensuring that sufficient funds are provided for such a purpose should be one part of a school's book-buying policy.

Because books are used throughout the school day and in all curriculum areas, another aim of such a policy should be to monitor the range, suitability and readability of the textbooks and information books in use with each age group. Subject specialists, when choosing textbooks and information books, need to take into consideration factors relating to the content, language, compellingness and format of the book and the way in which it would be used. Ideally a meeting of the subject department should be organised, with the language consultant and the remedial teacher present, to discuss the readability and suitability of books under consideration.

Readability

In choosing textbooks and information books to use with your students you will need some guide to their readability. Assessing the readability of a text is a difficult problem, since motivation is a key factor in determining whether or not a pupil will be able to cope with a particular text. Also, most readability tests are either complicated to conduct or simple but unreliable.

The following method of judging a text's

readability is adapted from Fry's readability graph, an American formula. The explanation of how to operate it is taken from the *BBC Adult literacy handbook*.

Method
● Select three separate 100-word passages, preferably at the beginning, middle and end of the material.

India after 1763

After the Peace of Paris, the East India Company was left in complete control of an enormous area of India, and, as a result, profits rose. Yet so much power had its disadvantages too, for the Company found itself deeply involved in Indian politics. Now the men who were sent to India were merchants and clerks, not statesmen. They could deal with cargoes and ledgers, but were quite out of their depth when it came to politics. The Indian princes were, moreover, men of great wealth, willing to pay to get their way. The result was that the Company officials found themselves exposed to temptations which were, as Clive said, 'such as flesh and blood could not be expected to withstand'. In short, bribes were offered and accepted, the administration was inefficient and dishonest and the Company servants grew rich. The Governor of Bengal, a Company servant, with an income of £4,000,000 a year and an army of 30,000, ruled 26,000,000 subjects. In 1770 there was a dreadful famine in Bengal, and the poverty of the people there seemed so great a contrast to the wealth of the Company that the government decided that some power would have to be taken from the Company.

In fact, two acts were passed, which left the Company free to trade, but brought the government of the country under the control of the British Government. In the meantime, Warren Hastings was sent out to Bengal, and he reformed the government and administration there. So suspicious were some politicians of all those who had ruled in India that even he was accused of dishonesty and oppression, and was only found not guilty after a trial lasting seven years. Still, he did not suffer in vain, for however ambitious and intolerant future British officials in India were, they were usually honest and efficient.

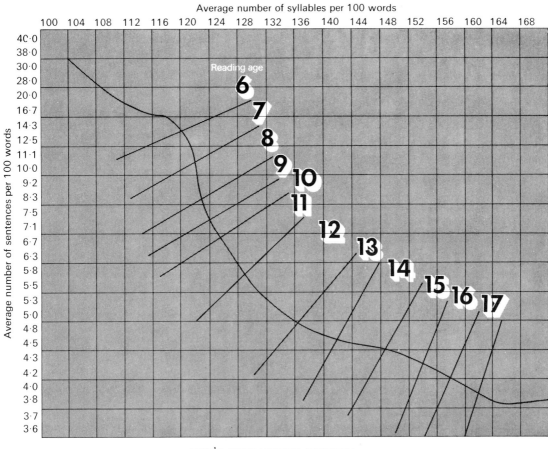

FRY'S READABILITY FORMULA

- In each passage find:
(a) the total number of syllables. The easiest pattern to adopt is to start with 100 (one syllable for each of the 100 words) and go through the passage adding on all the syllables in addition to the first syllable in each word.
(b) the total number of sentences.

- Average out the number of syllables and sentences for all three passages.

- Read off the graph above. The nearer the black line the more accurate the figure.

Suitability

Having established the readability of a book or piece of printed material ask yourself the questions (below) to establish further whether or not it is suitable for use with your class. You should ask yourself the same questions about any written material that you present to the class, e.g. your own worksheets.

Is the text compelling? Will a pupil find it immediately interesting and appealing?

How clearly are the facts/ideas put across? Is the

order of presentation straightforward? Are the facts/ideas easy to grasp?

How dense is the text? How many facts/ideas will the pupil reader encounter per paragraph? per page?

Is the level of abstraction and conceptual difficulty of the text suitable to the age, maturity and motivation of the pupils who will be expected to read it?

How complex is the style of the text? Is the sentence structure simple or are complicated grammatical structures used? if so, will the pupils be familiar with them?

How difficult is the vocabulary that is used? When specialist, technical terms are introduced are they adequately explained? Is there a glossary?

Are the pages well-designed with any illustrations/ diagrams suitably positioned in relation to the text? Are there too many pictures per page or perhaps too much text per page?

Is the print size too big or too small for the age and ability of the pupils who will use it?

Are the illustrations suitable to the age range with whom it will be used? Do they complement the text? Do they supplement it, adding an extra dimension to the section/chapter? Are they just decorative or perhaps even distracting?

If it is a textbook, are the activities suggested and the questions asked suitable? Are the questions open-ended or closed? Do they stimulate thought? Are any instructions that are given easy to follow?

How easy is it to find information from the book? Is there a table of contents? Is there an index? If so, is the book well indexed?

How would you use the book in class? To introduce the facts/ideas that it contains? To reinforce and summarise an oral lesson in which you have either

presented them or allowed the students to discover them for themselves?

Would you give it to the pupils to read on their own? in class? at home?

Finally, what claims do the publishers/authors make for the material? In the light of your examination are these claims justifiable?

It has been suggested that the textbooks and worksheets that we use in schools and the way that we use them is a key factor in discouraging many of our pupils from developing an interest in books and reading. *What do you think?*

The school library

Although school libraries are usually adequately stocked in terms of the number of books available, many of them are under-used. A school which has a library of several thousand books may have only between 100 and 200 out on loan at any time. How extensively the library is used depends on a number of factors. These include ease of access, the opportunities for browsing and borrowing both during regular library periods and outside lesson time, the extent to which teachers of all subjects offer guidance in the choice of books by accompanying pupils to the library and a simple system of borrowing that is flexible enough to tolerate a certain amount of forgetfulness. It depends too, of course, on the range and suitability of the books in stock. The choice of books is so important that at least one meeting of every subject department per year should be held in the library, with the language consultant and the head of the remedial department present. Current stock should be reviewed, new publications discussed and a suggested list of purchases drawn up.

How extensively is your school library used? What proportion of the books that are borrowed are

Meet Polly

Name:	Pauline Waters
Age:	fourteen years, three months
School:	girls' grammar
Offence:	stealing from an Oxford Street store, two cardigans and a pair of tights: value £4.70
Place of trial:	juvenile court

By stealing Polly has broken the law, been arrested by the police and prosecuted by another citizen (the store manager) for committing a crime.

Alan, probably, is a special case and because of his home background, etc., is lik[ely] to belong to that small class of persistent offenders despite efforts by everybody conc[erned]. On this occasion he was committed for ap[proved] school training. As the superintendent, M[r ...] wrote to me:

'It is so sad, you will agree, but we must remember that he *was* a menace to soc[iety]. [At] ten years of age he may well respond t[o ...] and make the grade when he eventual[ly returns] to society. Everything of course will d[epend on] the home background and the suppor[t he will] receive in the home setting.'

But what about somebody like Po[lly,] first offender. Will she join the 70 p[er cent of] people who come before a court ar[e never to] reappear? We'll follow her case thr[ough. But] first *what is a crime?*

20

What is a crime?

English law is divided into two main sections: **criminal law**, which deals largely with offences for which people can be punished and **civil law**, which concerns disputes between two or more people and which usually has nothing to do with the question of punishment.

So, we can give a technical definition of what a crime is:

'Any action or omission, punishable by a penalty, which only the Sovereign in the exercise of the Royal Prerogative of mercy may pardon or remit.'

From *The Criminal Law* by F. T. Giles

But it is much easier, and free from squabble, to say simply –

'[... an] offence punishable in a [...]'

What is Crime?

in thousands

Offences known to the police

2 000

1 500

1 000

500

1951 1961 1966 1969 1970 1971 1972

The simplest definition of a crime is an offence or an act which is punishable in a criminal court. In the 1970s, the number of offences known to the police has been between one and a half and two millions each year. The situation seems even gloomier when we consider that, in addition to this, we must include the 'Dark Number' of crimes—the many offences which never come to the attention of the police and for which we can only guess a number.

But let us look a little more closely at the word 'crime'. All of us at times, either accidentally or deliberately, have committed offences—broken laws, many of which were made many years ago and no longer apply to the age we live in.

All of the points in the article (left) show laws or local regulations (by-laws) being broken—most of them could not be called serious and yet if the police had the time and the desire, they could prosecute each of the offenders.

How many laws will you break today?

A SPECIAL REPORT

The truth is (luckily for us!) that there's too much law to be enforced. As I walked from Waterloo to Holborn, looking for violations of the Laws of England, I saw....

(a) A girl feeding the pigeons inside Waterloo Station.
(b) Two cars with expired Excise licences.
(c) Three cars with none at all.
(d) Twenty-three cars parked on the footway.
(e) One flag-day girl shaking a collecting box in people's faces.
(f) A cycling window cleaner carrying a ladder on his shoulder.
(g) A painter on a window sill wearing no means of preventing a fall.

fiction? Does your library contain a wide enough range of both quality and non-quality fiction to cater for the needs and interests of pupils of all abilities?

Is the system of borrowing easy? Does it encourage or discourage the less-motivated pupils to take out books?

Do your pupils have regular library lessons? Do teachers of all subjects accompany pupils to the library?

Who is responsible for buying books for your school library? Are there regular meetings to review the stock and to discuss new publications?

Resources for use with the slow learner

Structured schemes

Griffin and Dragon Pirate stories E. J. Arnold, 1970–72.
A comprehensive scheme of 52 books, 12 complementary workcards and assorted support materials – flashcards, cassette recordings, dominoes, wall pictures, picture and work plaques and an 'I Spy' book. Particularly useful with boys. By Sheila McCullagh.

Help! Nelson.
A language development course for 10–14-year-olds with reading ages 6–8. Graded into 6 levels, each with a preliminary reader, a story book, an extension reader and a workbook. Lively stories providing a mixture of adventure, humour and suspense. Also 16 spirit masters presenting graded story outlines. By James Webster.

Men of the west Good Reading.
A complete literacy programme, consisting of 10 cassettes, story cards, worksheets and games. Its cowboy-and-Indian content make it most useful with boys. By Ruth Nichols.

Racing to read E. J. Arnold.
A language development kit, consisting of 12 books, workcards, 2 workbooks, games and cassette recordings. Uses a carefully graded vocabulary of 200 words plus 109 made by compounding known words. Together with *Sound sense* forms an integrated scheme, but can also be used successfully with other schemes. By A. E. Tansley and R. H. Nicholls.

Remedial reading workshop Ward Lock.
A kit of 100 workcards and 100 answer cards, graded in a colour code sequence, prepared by S. H. Wrench and Donald Moyle. Designed for 10–14-year-olds with reading ages of 6 years 8 months to 9 years.

Sound sense E. J. Arnold, n.e. 1971.
Seven books and a teacher's book, written by A. E. Tansley. A systematic phonic approach.

Stott programmed reading kit Holmes McDougall, 1962.
A comprehensive scheme of 29 aids and games for the teaching of reading and phonics which can be used alongside any reading scheme. Prepared by D. H. Stott. Most useful with 8–12-year-olds but can be used with older pupils.

Support materials

The structured schemes are more suited to younger pupils aged 10–13 than to older pupils. They are most effective when used in conjunction with reading games and other reading activities and supplementary readers. An increasing number of games, such as the Betty Root reading games (Good Reading) and the Betty Root card games (Hart-Davis), have become available in recent years. Both Good Reading Ltd and James Galt and Co. produce a wide range and it is worth consulting their catalogues. Similarly Philip and Tacey market a useful selection of reading activity materials.

When choosing a game for use in the classroom ask yourself:

Does it extend the child's reading? Is suitable reinforcement provided?

Are the correct responses rewarded? Is it self-corrective?

The slow learner, 14-16

Often the best way of starting with an older secondary pupil is to make your own materials.

The section on reading materials in Herbert Kohl's *Reading, how to* (Penguin Books, 1975) contains a wealth of suggestions. It is also worth consulting the *BBC Adult literacy handbook*, since the approaches you adopt with 14–16-year-olds, who have failed to learn to read, must be similar to those you would use with an adult.

Reading series for older slow learners

Approach trend Ginn, 1976.
These books in the popular Australian *Trend* series provide suitable easy readers for older secondary pupils. Titles include *Vroom! Vroom!*, *Night cats!* and *Walk in the sun*.

Club books, Disco books Cassell, 1975.
Two series of slim paperback booklets, telling very short stories in simple language on topics such as dating, starting work and running away from home. Disco books by Joan Tate. Club books by Joan Tate, A. L. and D. S. Higgins, A. Ramsay and Irma Chilton.

Heinemann guided readers (Beginner level), 1973–5.
Designed for immigrants and foreign learners. Concise plots with plenty of action. Reading age 8. Vocabulary 700 words. Titles such as *Death of a soldier* by Philip Prowse and *Money for a motorbike* by John Milne.

Jim Hunter books Methuen, 1975.
Four escapist adventure stories by Ben Butterworth and Bill Stockdale about special agent Jim Hunter, his dog Radar and their struggles with the master criminal Bratt. The first two books with 'cinematic illustrations' and 'bubble texts' lead on to two longer stories with caption texts.

The Manxman and *The raft on the river* Dent, 1972–3.
Two sets of 6 stories by Cliff Edwards, presented in comic form. The *Manxman* books centre round a motorcycle; *The raft on the river* series includes *Making kayaks* and *A big fish*.

The marriage scene Collins, 1975.
A series of 8 books focussing on a young married couple and how they cope with a variety of situations. A resource pack containing a tape, slides and a teacher's book by Clifford Parfit is also available.

Seekers Special Educational Publications, 1973.
Three books by Cliff Parfit about a footballer – *Tony gets a chance*; a pop group – *Ray's dream*; a babysitting incident – *Mum's night out*.

Solos Hart-Davis Educational, 1974.
Eight stories on themes of interest to teenagers by Kathleen Wood, including *All the long night* about anxious parents waiting for their son to come home, *Sixth sense*, the story of a girl with extra-sensory perception, and *Five miles from Fenbury* about a girl who takes a baby.

Stories for today Heinemann Educational, 1972–4.
Twelve titles, nine by Peter Abbs, e.g. *Ginger and Sharon, The big game*. Simple sentences, but quite advanced vocabulary. The three books by Carol Bergman, *Donnovan, Paul* and *Naomi*, may be particularly useful with multi-racial classes.

Waxwell books Grail Publications.
Five stories about Ken, how he finds a job and meets Sally. Each book is self-contained, although the vocabulary builds up from only 91 words in book one. Titles include *A night out*,

The weekend, written and illustrated by
Kathleen Berman.

Books for slow learners
Note The books listed in this section can be used
with slow readers as supplementary readers,
alongside the materials mentioned in the
previous section.

For 10–13-year-olds
Adventures in space Hart-Davis Educational,
1968–70.
Four simply written space adventures by
Sheila McCullagh, each of which is told in
separate instalments in 3 books.

The Brick Street boys Armada Picture Lions,
1976.
Simple lively stories by Allan and Janet Ahlberg
about the Brick Street boys and their football
games. Humorous text and illustrations.
Extremely popular with boys.

Banjo books Cassell, 1975; 3 sets of 4 vols. each.
Adventure stories by G. R. Crosher, D. A. Cliffe
and A. L. and D. S. Higgins. Titles include *A
match on the patch*, *Dead on time* and *No time to
scream*. Useful also with reluctant readers.

Club 75 Macmillan, 1975.
Eighteen titles in a bright attractive format, each
of approximately 7500 words. Authors include
Alan Plater, Irma Chilton, Barry Pointon and
Albert Rowe. High quality illustrations by
artists like Trevor Stubley and Gareth Floyd.
Useful too with reluctant readers and older slow
learners. General editor Aidan Chambers.

Contact Collins, 1975.
Action-packed stories by Michael Hardcastle,
illustrated by Gareth Floyd. Eight titles, e.g.

Road race, *Dead of night*, *The match*. *First
contact* provides another four titles for a slightly
younger interest level.

Crown Street Kings Macmillan, 1972–5.
Eighteen stories about the noisy, happy King
family written in a colloquial style with a
phonetic bias and constant repetition, by Anne
Oates. Cartoon-style illustrations and lively text.

Go readers Blond, 1964.
Four stories by Martin Calman about young
teenage boys: *Ron's first round*, *Ted makes a
splash*, *What about Fred?* and *Can Fred ride?*

Headlines Edward Arnold, 1977.
Four books each containing 5 true stories of
approximately 1200 words that can be read by
those with a reading age of 8–10 within 20 or 30
minutes. Includes *Daredevils*, stories of Evel
Knievel, a lion-tamer, a sword-swallower,
Houdini and a film stuntman, *Remarkable
animals*, *Survivors from the sea* and *Record-
breakers*. Can also be used with older slow
learners. General editor John L. Foster.

Inner ring books Benn, cased and paperback,
1965 to date.
Stories about teenagers in a city setting by Alan
Pullen and Cyril Rapstoff (first series), Michael
Hardcastle (second series) and Helen Cresswell
(third series). Also *Inner ring sports*, 8 books by
David Clarke on football, swimming and table-
tennis; *Inner ring true stories* by Moyra
Hamilton, about spies, exploration, the sea and
escape; and *Inner ring facts*, by Frank Knight
and James Stuart, 2 books on aeroplanes and
ships. Can also be used effectively with some
older pupils.

Ladder books OUP, 1976.
Information books, useful for topic and project

work, with the material organised into concise and distinct sections and a paragraph indexing system that can be used to teach children how to use an index and to find information.

Five titles: *Birds, Space and space travel, Famous names, War and warriors* and *Land travel*. Series editor Olive Robinson.

Lively reading Nelson, 1973.
A series of 16 information books and 4 workbooks by Leonard Sealey, with carefully controlled vocabulary and full-colour illustrations on every page, and 4 accompanying workbooks. Subjects include *Man on the moon, Car racing, Test pilot* and *Earthquakes and volcanoes*.

Patchwork paperbacks Cassell, 1974–6.
An Australian series, 3 sets of 4 vols. Some of the stories, therefore, have only a limited appeal. Contains two good science fiction stories by Lee Harding, *The fallen spaceman* and *The frozen sky*, that are useful also with reluctant readers. Series editor Barry Carozzi.

Rescue reading Ginn, 1968–75.
Consists of *Rescue stories*, simple well-written stories in which an animal plays a large part; *More rescue stories*, which are slightly more difficult; and *Rescue adventures*, exciting adventures about burglars, smugglers, forest fires and spacemen. All by James Webster.

Tempo books Longman, 1965–7.
Ten books by Paul Groves and Leslie Stratta each containing stories about the activities and adventures of a brother and sister and their friends. The situations described are within the experience of 10–13-year-olds, e.g. *Bonfire night, At the market, The fair*. Lists in each book enable you to see the vocabulary extent of each story.

Trend Ginn, 1976.
Over 30 titles in a graded series that originated in Australia. Extremely useful, but the books vary enormously in difficulty and you need to check carefully to ensure that you have chosen one at the appropriate level. Their content makes them suitable for use throughout the 10–16 age range.

For 13–16-year-olds
Anchor books Cassell, 1973–6.
Eight titles including four adventure-type stories from G. R. Crosher and two about boy-meets-girl situations – *Polly and the barrow boy* by Joan Tate and *When the song was over* by Anna Higgins.

Encounter Cassell, 1977.
For those with a reading age of 11–12. Six books, first published in Australia, including *Flop and Mick and John and me*, short stories about four boys, *Debbie's guy* and *The children of Atlantis*, a science fiction story by Lee Harding. Series editor Barry Carozzi.

Focus Blackie, 1970–3.
Ten adventure stories by George Kee about four teenagers – Carol, Liz, Bill and Joe. Each book poses some problem of everyday life and there are suggestions for group discussion work.

Heinemann guided readers, 1973.
Books at 4 levels – some original stories, some simplified versions of popular modern novels such as *Shane, The pearl* and *Old Mali and the boy*. Carefully graded vocabulary and structure, designed for foreign learners but can be useful with the older child, especially Philip Prowse's adventure thrillers *Bristol murder* and *The woman who disappeared*. Series editor John Milne.

Inswinger, Popswinger Hulton Educational, 1973–4.
Two sets of six books – *Inswinger* about the football career of young Les Barnes, *Popswinger* about the career of a pop group. The basic vocabulary in *Inswinger 1* is 460 words and is added to gradually at the rate of about 200 words per book. By Gerald Gregory and Ritchie Ward.

The Mark Kent stories Oliver and Boyd, 1975.
Exciting adventure stories by Hendy Smith charting the army career of Mark Kent from raw recruit via assignments in various parts of the world to the winning of a medal and the rank of sergeant. Four of the five stories are available on cassettes.

The motivation reader Methuen, 1976.
Hard-cover books by J. F. Stevens, with a half-page colour photograph on each page and a text of no more than 50 words, giving introductions to 4 lesser known sports – *Water skiing, Trail bike riding, Hang-gliding* and *Sailing skiffs*.

Read, write and enjoy – Speedway series Oliver and Boyd, 1975–6.
Three separate books by P. Westwood, which together make up a full-length novel, about a boy starting work, entering the world of speedway, falling in love and getting married.

Sprint books Nelson, 1975.
Stories for older teenagers arranged in 4 packs, Pack 1 containing those of particular interest to girls, Pack 2 those to appeal to boys and Packs 3 and 4 those of interest to both boys and girls. Pocket-sized format and comic-quality illustrations. By Tom Speed and Elsie Spence.

Trigger Collins, 1975.
Eight stories, ranging in quality, on subjects such as boxing, football, pop and motor-cycles, by various authors.

Books for reluctant readers

Note. Some 10–16-year-olds become reluctant readers because they do not have the reading stamina to sustain the concentration required to handle books of the length of an average children's novel. Many of the books from the series mentioned as suitable for underachieving readers can also be useful with reluctant readers who fall into this category.

For 10–13-year-olds

Inner ring red circle hipsters Benn, 1976.
Four stories about Dave, Stringer, Linda and Mag, with plenty of incident and humour. Written by Richard Parker, illustrated by Trevor Stubley.

Instant reading Heinemann, 1970–1.
A series of 10 books by W. C. H. Chalk. Five of them are humorous tales about Skinny Willy and his friends at the school at Ash Green, including one about a robot, *The Iron Man*. *Jim Silent* is about an Indian, while the other four are not-too-demanding science-fiction stories: *The terrible things, The firebirds, The moonlanders* and *The conquest of Mars*. A very popular series of lively stories.

Knockouts Longman, 1976–.
Most of the titles published so far in this series are more suitable for older readers. Jan Carew's short stories about the supernatural, *Save the last dance for me*, and about the future, *Stranger than tomorrow*, are, however, simply enough written for this age group as is John Christopher's *In the beginning*. Also, George Layton's stories,

A northern childhood, are very popular with upper primary and lower secondary children.

Onward paperbacks Cassell, 1973 and 1976. Adventure stories by G. R. Crosher. Set 1 consists of *A bomb in the submarine*, *Ken and the kidnappers*, *Hideout* and *Hunt the necklace*.

Rockets Macmillan, 1977. Stories by authors such as Petronella Breinburg, Ray Jenkins, Aidan Chambers and Irma Chilton. The first 8 titles include science-fiction, western and animal stories as well as realistic, contemporary ones. General editor Aidan Chambers.

Spirals Hutchinson, 1976. Six short stories of the supernatural by Anita Jackson, which have a wide appeal because of their subject matter, and because they are simple enough to be read by anyone who has just learned to read and short enough to attract those who are competent but reluctant to try longer books.

Topliners Macmillan, 1968. Most titles in this series are more suitable for older pupils, but a few have a wide appeal to children in the upper primary and middle school. These are the books about Louie and Birdy Jones by E. W. Hildick, Roy Wilson's two football stories about Danny Martin, *First season* and *Season in Europe*, Reginald Maddock's *The dragon in the garden*, *The pit* and *Sell out* and Christine Dickenson's *Dark horse*.

Tracker books Carousel, 1972–3. An ingenious series, giving the reader the chance to build up his own version of the story by offering him a choice of directions at particular points in the book. Comic-style pictures and fast-moving adventure stories such as *Mission to planet L*, *Secret of the seventh star*, *Codebreaker* and *Skyjacked* by S. Leslie, K. James and J. Allen.

For 14–16-year-olds
Booster books Heinemann, 1967. Ten stories with quickly developing plots by W. C. H. Chalk including a spy mystery, a wartime thriller, an historical romance of the sea. Also, 3 science-fiction stories, *The man from Mars*, *Mask of dust* and the very popular *The Gnomids*, the tale of the strange monkey-like creatures who appear from under the earth and threaten man's survival. This series can also be enjoyed by younger readers who have the ability and the stamina to cope with the text.

Bull's-eye Hutchinson, 1975. Adaptations of popular adult novels by authors such as Ian Fleming, John Wyndham, Victor Canning, Hammond Innes and Dennis Wheatley. Series editor Patrick Nobes.

Checkers Evans, 1974. Three sets (4 titles) of specially written stories by B. Boyers, E. Owen and others around the themes of authority, family relationships and sport. Simple, undemanding stories, not very attractively illustrated.

Getaway Nelson, 1977. Twenty-four titles, including fast-moving undemanding stories by Michael Hardcastle and Geoffrey Baker, 3 westerns by William Hurst and 3 historical novels by Rony Robinson, and collections of science-fiction and mystery and suspense stories. Also *Gangs and victims*, short stories by Joan Tate, Evan Hunter, Shelagh Delaney and others.

Interest books Nelson, 1973. Mostly non-fiction books. *Starters 1–4* by Rod

Hunt are compilations of stories and articles on topics such as Jack Sheppard the jailbreaker, UFOs, weddings and Ned Kelly. Other books include *Football champions*, *Athletics champions* and *Inventors and scientists*.

Joan Tate books Heinemann, 1964–70.
Eighteen titles, most of which are suitable for 14–16-year-olds, though a few appeal more to younger pupils. Stories range from those about a girl's first holiday abroad and a girl from the West Indies coming to terms with life in England to the sensitive portrayal of a relationship between a boy who is very withdrawn and the girl with whom he at last manages to make contact in *The tree*.

Knockouts Longman, 1976–.
A broad range of fiction written at several levels of difficulty, clearly indicated by the colouring of the books and spines. It includes Janet Green's controversial gang stories, *The six*, the widely-acclaimed *Mia* by Gunnel Beckman, Bruce Carter's *The bike racers*, S. E. Hinton's *Rumble fish*, and 5 books by Joan Tate. Series editor Josie Levine.

Pyramids Heinemann, 1967–.
Immensely popular hardback series, essential in the school library. Stories of all kinds ranging from romance for the girls, e.g. Pamela Sykes's *East, west*, Dorothy Clewes's *Ginny's boy*, to suspense and adventure for the boys, e.g. Jack Ronder's *Mouse code* and Roy Wilson's *One long Sunday*. Books by many other established authors such as Prudence Andrew, Honor Arundel, Aidan Chambers, Geraldine Kaye, Jean Macgibbon and Richard Parker.

Topliners Macmillan, 1968–.
Unquestionably the most popular of the reluctant reader series. Offers a wide variety of stories – football, science fiction, love, thrillers, teenage and contemporary problems and ghosts – varying in difficulty and in quality. Popular titles include *The contender*, *That's love*, *Ghosts 2*, *Sam and me* and *Escape on Monday*. *Topliner redstars* aim to take the reluctant reader on to more demanding books, but some of the initial titles have proved rather too difficult for many younger *Topliner* readers. General editor Aidan Chambers.

Miscellaneous

The following books not in any of the above series, have also proved popular with older reluctant readers:

ARUNDEL, H. *Emma in love* H. Hamilton, 1970; Piccolo, 1973.
BALLARD, M. *Dockie* Kestrel, 1972; Armada Lions, 1974.
BANKS, L. R. *My darling villain* Bodley Head, 1977.
BARSTOW, S. *Joby* Heinemann, 1971; Corgi, 1973.
BORISOFF, N. *You might even like it* Scholastic, 1976.
CHAMBERS, A. *Haunted houses* Piccolo, 1971.
CONE, M. *The real dream* Scholastic, 1976.
DALY, M. *Sixteen and other stories* Scholastic, 1976.
EVANS, A. *Running scared* Brockhampton Press, 1975; Beaver 1977
FALK, A. M. *A place of her own* Scholastic, 1976.
GLANVILLE, B. *Goalkeepers are different* H. Hamilton, 1971; Puffin Books, 1974.
GLANVILLE, B. *The Puffin book of football* Puffin Books, 1970.
HINES, B. *A kestrel for a knave* (*Kes*) Pergamon Press, 1969; Penguin Books, 1969.
KAMM, J. *Young mother* Brockhampton Press, 1975; Heinemann, 1968.

KAMM, J. *The starting point* Brockhampton Press, 1975.

LEESON, R. *The third class genie* Armada Lions, 1975.

MCGRATH, P. *The green leaves of Nottingham* Hutchinson, 1973.

MILDINER, L. and HOUSE, B. *The gates* Centerprise, 1975.

POINTON, B. *Cave* Bodley Head, 1976.

PRICE, S. *Sticks and stones* Faber, 1976.

SHERBURNE, Z. *The girl who knew tomorrow* Scholastic, 1976.

SHERRY, S. *A pair of Jesus boots* Cape, 1969; Heinemann, 1975; Puffin Books, 1973.

SUDBERY, R. *Rich and famous and bad* Deutsch, 1970; Carousel, 1972.

WESTALL, R. *The machine-gunners* Macmillan, 1975; Puffin, 1977.

WOOD, K. *Gulls* Dobson, 1974.

ZINDEL, P. *My darling, my hamburger* Bodley Head, 1970; Corgi, 1974.

Books and materials for extending and developing reading skills

Reading laboratories

A number of these are widely used in schools. They can be stored easily, are simple to use with a large class and keep the pupils occupied. All too often they become a routine, keeping the pupils busy rather than extending them, and providing a substitute for the more demanding task involved in silent reading followed by group-discussion activities.

Within the context of a well-developed reading programme it is possible that they may have a part to play. But it must be remembered that reading cards and answering multiple-choice questions are not the only reading activities that pupils should be engaged in during the time set aside for their reading and that reading laboratories, if used, must be used alongside books, if the reading habit is to be acquired.

What claims are made for reading laboratories? What evidence is there to support these claims?

Are the criticisms that many teachers make of reading laboratories justified? How, when and why might you use a reading laboratory in your programme?
(See also part 2, page 27.)

Your own materials

In the absence of suitable published materials designed to develop and extend reading skills, it is often necessary to produce your own. Passages and stories taken from newspapers and magazines can be cut into sections and used for group prediction and group sequencing activities. Similarly you can prepare your own passages for group cloze work. Deletions can be every fifth, seventh or tenth word depending on the passage's difficulty and the age and ability of the pupils. With difficult passages it is best not to start deletions until about the hundredth word.
(See also part 2, page 27.)

Short stories

These can be used for group prediction work by reading them aloud to the class and pausing for discussion at suitable points. Similarly they can be used for comparative purposeful reading, either by giving groups of pupils different questions to discuss and then inviting them to share their thoughts, or by asking them to read a story and then prepare their own questions on it. In the latter case groups can write their answers to other groups' questions. They can then be 'marked' and the questions and answers discussed.

Collections of stories suitable for class use include:

For 10–13-year-olds

BARRY, M. S. *Tommy Mac* Kestrel, 1972; Puffin, 1974.

FOSTER, J. L. ed. *Escapades* Edward Arnold, 1976.

GARFIELD, L. ed. *Baker's dozen* Ward Lock, 1974; Piccolo, 1976.

JACKSON, D. ed. *Springboard* Harrap, 1970.

JACKSON, D. and PEPPER, D. eds. *The blue storyhouse* OUP, 1976.

JACKSON, D. and PEPPER, D. eds. *The green storyhouse* OUP, 1976.

LAYTON, G. *A northern childhood* Longman, paperback, 1976.

MARLAND, M. ed. *First choice* Longman, 1961.

NAUGHTON, B. *The goalkeeper's revenge* Heinemann, 1974; Puffin Books, 1970.

PEARCE, P. *What the neighbours did* Kestrel, 1972; Puffin Books, 1975.

For 14–16-year-olds

ADAMS, A. et al. *Storymakers* 1–3 Harrap, 1974.

BARNES, D. and EGFORD, R. eds. *Twentieth century short stories* Harrap, 1959.

BENNETT, B. et al. *Spectrum* 1–2 Longman, 1971.

HOLBROOK, D. *People and diamonds* 1 and 2 CUP, 1962.

HUNTER, J. ed. *Modern short stories* Faber, 1964.

HUNTER, J. ed. *The human animal* Faber, 1973.

JACKSON, D. and PEPPER, D. *Story* 1–3 Penguin Books, 1973.

THOMPSON, D. and PARRY, C. eds. *Leopards* series A and B CUP, 1972.

Series:

Imprint books Gen. editor M. MARLAND. Longman.

Literature for life Gen. editor K. CALTHROP. Wheaton.

Pegasus Harrap.

WLE short stories Gen. editor J. L. FOSTER. Ward Lock.

The class reader

Class readers have a useful part to play in developing the reader's response by offering a shared experience, provided that unprepared reading round the class is avoided and that the follow-up activities in the middle and lower secondary school are imaginative and creative, and that literary critical essay work is not introduced too early. Ideas for creative writing and drama work on a number of novels can be found in *Reading study units* by J. Foster, Heinemann, 1974.

Books suitable for use as class readers include:

BALDWIN, M. *Grandad with snails* Hutchinson, 1971.

BARSTOW, S. *Joby* M. Joseph, 1964; Heinemann, 1971; Corgi, 1973.

BATES, H. E. *Fair stood the wind for France* M. Joseph, 1964; Longman, 1971; Penguin Books, 1970.

BRAITHWAITE, E. R. *To sir, with love* Heinemann, 1970; Bodley Head, 1959; Blackie, 1974; NEL, 1969.

CHRISTOPHER, J. *The guardians* H. Hamilton, 1970; Heinemann, 1975; Puffin Books, 1973.

FOX, P. *The slave dancer* Piccolo, 1977.

GARNER, A. *Elidor* Armada, 1965.

GOLDING, W. *Lord of the flies* Faber, cased and paperback, 1954.

HEMINGWAY, E. *The old man and the sea* Cape, 1952; Panther, 1976.

HINES, B. *A kestrel for a knave (Kes)* Pergamon Press, 1969; Penguin Books, 1969.

HOLM, A. *I am David* Methuen, 1965; Puffin Books, 1969.

LEE, H. *To kill a mockingbird* Heinemann, 1960; Pan, 1974.

MARSHALL, J. V. *Walkabout* Penguin Books, 1969.

MARSHALL, J. V. *A river ran out of Eden* Hodder and Stoughton, 1962; Heinemann, 1971.
NAUGHTON, B. *A dog called Nelson* Dent, 1976.
ORWELL, G. *Animal farm* various editions.
SCHAEFER, J. *Shane* Heinemann, 1957; Deutsch, 1963; Penguin Books, 1969.
SCHAEFER, J. *The canyon* Deutsch, 1955; Heinemann, 1963; Corgi, 1975.
SERRAILLIER, I. *The silver sword* Heinemann, 1951; Cape, 1956; Puffin Books, 1970.
SHERMAN, D. R. *Old Mali and the boy* Heinemann, 1973; Penguin Books, 1968.
SHERRY, S. *A pair of Jesus boots* Heinemann, 1975; Puffin Books, 1973.
SPERRY, A. *The boy who was afraid* Heinemann, 1952; Bodley Head, 1963; Knight Books, 1967.
STEINBECK, J. *The pearl* Heinemann, 1954; Pan, 1970.
STEINBECK, J. *Of mice and men* Heinemann, 1965; Pan, 1974.
STEINBECK, J. *The red pony* Heinemann, 1961; Piccolo, 1975.
TAYLOR, T. *The cay* Bodley Head, 1970; Heinemann, 1973.
WALSH, J. P. *Fireweed* Macmillan, 1969; Puffin Books, 1972.
WELLS, H. G. *The time machine* Heinemann, 1895; Pan, 1968.
WRIGHTSON, P. *I own the racecourse* Hutchinson, 1968; Puffin Books, 1977.
WYNDHAM, J. *The day of the triffids* M. Joseph, 1951; Hutchinson, 1975; Penguin Books, 1970.

Drama

Drama activities – improvisation, role play, scriptwriting, play reading, tape-recording and play production – are an important way of extending pupils' language by providing opportunities for a wide range of talk and reading. With 10–13-year-olds drama work can often be integrated with English work centred around a theme or topic. Older pupils can be

prepared for 'O' level or CSE Mode 1 Drama examinations or you can, if you prefer to do so, submit your own CSE Mode 3 'Theatre Arts', 'Media Studies' or 'Drama' syllabus. You can find out about existing examinations from the GCE and CSE boards.

Workshop materials
ADLAND, D. E. *The group approach to drama* Books 1–6 Longman, 1964–72.
Situations and story-outlines to stimulate group activities with 11–15-year-olds.

BOWSKILL, D. *Workshop one: circus, fairground, zoo* Dent, 1974.
A multi-media kit consisting of a teachers' book, a tape, a filmstrip and a pupils' book.

FOSTER, J. L. *Against the odds* Nelson, 1976.
Dramatic assignments giving 11–13-year-olds

the opportunity to invent and act out the type of adventure stories that capture their imagination.

MARTIN, W. and VALLINS, G. *Exploration drama* Evans, 1968.
Four books – *Carnival, Legend, Horizon* and *Routes* – using extracts from literary, artistic and historical sources as stimuli for drama work with 11–13-year-olds.

NORRIS, J. and EVANS, M. *Drama resource cards* Longman, 1977.
Eighty cards including session cards giving lesson outlines, 'how to do it' cards and drama games. For use with lower secondary students.

PORTER, S. *Action pack* Edward Arnold, 1977.
Forty-eight cards graded into 3 levels of difficulty for use with 9–14-year-olds.

THOMSON, P. and GOODHEAD, C. *Ideas in action* 3 Hodder and Stoughton, 1976.
Nine projects for use with 13- and 14-year-olds.

WATCYN-JONES, P. and J. *Think, move, speak: a drama workcard series* Hodder and Stoughton, 1975.
Practical, well-tried suggestions for use with 10–13-year-olds. Set 1 Mime and movement. Set 2 Stories for acting. Set 3 Improvisation.

YATES, P. and HORNBY, R. *Ideas in action* 1 and 2 Hodder and Stoughton, 1974.
Stimulus material for use with 11- and 12-year-olds.

Ideally you need a drama studio or a large open space for your drama sessions, but many of the ideas suggested in these books and cards can be adapted for use in the ordinary classroom, where opportunities for acting out are restricted. Tapes and records and suitable lighting can help enormously to create atmosphere. A number of very useful records of sound effects and electronic music are available from BBC Enterprises, Villiers House, The Broadway, London W5 2PA.

Playscripts

Underachieving readers, slow learners and reluctant readers frequently enjoy reading books of plays more than they do other books, because they find the presentation of a text in play form less daunting. Often they are required to read only a short speech rather than a paragraph of several sentences and the chances of failure are, therefore, greatly reduced. They also get a lot of enjoyment, as well as reading practice, if you ask them to tape-record a one-act play or a scene from a full-length play.

For underachieving readers

FOSTER, J. L. et al. *Take a part* Nelson, 1973.
GROVES, P. and GRIMSHAW, N. *Join the action* Edward Arnold, 1973; *Action replay* Edward Arnold, 1975; *Action stations* Edward Arnold, 1976.
HOUNSEL-ROBERT, K. *The case of Kate Webster* Macmillan, 1973.
ROBINSON, R. *Down your way* Nelson, 1974.

For 10–14-year-olds

AIKEN, J. *Winterthing* and *The mooncusser's daughter* Cape, 1973; Puffin Books, 1975.
BOLT, R. *The thwarting of Baron Bolligrew* Heinemann, 1966; S. French, 1969.
CHAMBERS, A. *Johnny Salter* Heinemann, 1966; *The Car* Heinemann, 1967; *The chicken run* Heinemann, 1968.
CHARLESWORTH, J. *Tom Sawyer* Macmillan, 1976.
COFFEY, D. *The incredible vanishing* Eyre Methuen, 1975.
DICKENS, C. *Pip and the convict* ed. by G. R. Williams, Macmillan, 1971.
GARDINER, J. *The Dracula spectacula* Evans, 1976.
HALL, W. *Kidnapped at Christmas* Heinemann, 1975; S. French, 1975. *Christmas crackers* Heinemann, 1976.

POWNALL, D. *The dream of Chief Crazy Horse* Faber, cased and paperback 1975.
YATES, P. *Onward to the Oregon* Hodder and Stoughton, 1975.

For reluctant readers 14–16
BARSTOW, S. *A kind of loving* Blackie 1976.
BARSTOW, S. *Joby* Blackie, 1976.
BRIGHOUSE, H. *Hobson's choice* Heinemann, 1964; S. French, 1966.
BRITTIN, A. *The Mignonette* Macmillan, 1973.
CAMPBELL, K. *Jack Sheppard* Macmillan, 1976.
DELANEY, S. *A taste of honey* Eyre Methuen, 1974.
HALL, W. *The long and the short and the tall* Evans, 1959; Heinemann, 1965.
HALL, W. and WATERHOUSE, K. *Billy liar* Evans, 1960; Blackie, 1967.
HINES, B. and STRONACH, A. *Kes* Heinemann, 1973.
HODGSON, H. *Adam's ark* Macmillan, 1975.
LAURENTS, A. and SONDHEIM, S. *West side story* Heinemann, 1972.
NAUGHTON, B. *Spring and port wine* Heinemann, 1973.
OCTAGON THEATRE-IN-EDUCATION *Sweetie pie* Eyre Methuen, 1975.
OWEN, B. *The laundry girls* Macmillan, 1973.
PICK, J. *Carrigan Street* Macmillan, 1972.
PLATER, A. *You and me* Blackie, 1973.
PRIESTLEY, J. B. *An inspector calls* Heinemann, 1965.
RECKORD, B. *Skyvers* in *New English dramatists* 9 Penguin Books, 1966.
SPEAKMAN, R. and NICHOLLS, D. *Baker's boy* Macmillan, 1976.
TERSON, P. *Zigger Zagger* Penguin Books, 1970.
THOMAS, D. *The doctor and the devils* Macmillan, 1969.
WESKER, A. *Chips with everything* Blackie, 1976.

Series:
Conflict in drama 1 and 2 ed. J. Hodgson, Methuen, 1972.
Dramascripts Advisory ed. G. Williams, Macmillan, 1970–.
Hereford plays Gen. ed. E. R. Wood, Heinemann, 1965–.
Playbill 1–3 ed. A. Durband, Hutchinson, 1969–73.
Prompt 1–3 ed. A. Durband, Hutchinson, 1976.
Student drama Gen. ed. M. Marland, Blackie, 1967.

Television scripts

Several collections of television scripts are available in the Imprint series published by Longman. *Scene scripts* and *Z Cars scripts* in particular are suitable for use with older less motivated pupils. The film of *Last bus*, a script by Keith Dewhurst included in *Scene scripts*, can be hired from BBC Enterprises, Villiers House, The Broadway, London W5 2PA, who will send you a catalogue giving full details of other television programmes on film available for purchase or hire. Similarly, an extract from a *Z Cars* programme can be hired from the British Film Institute, 42/3 Lower Marsh, London SE1. Another collection, *The pressures of life*, contains the scripts of two plays that are currently included in the TV drama unit of the schools television series, *The English Programme*.

Television scripts suitable for use with older pupils include:

GALTON, A. and SIMPSON, R. *Steptoe and Son* Longman, 1971.
HOPKINS, J. *Talking to a stranger* Penguin Books, 1967. op.
JONES, E. *Softly, softly* Longman, 1976
MARLAND, M. ed. *Scene scripts* Longman, 1973.
MARLAND, M. ed. *Z Cars: four tv scripts* Longman, 1968.

MARLAND, M. ed. *The pressures of life* Longman, 1977.

MARLAND, M. ed. *Conflicting generations: five tv plays* Longman, 1968.

OWEN, A. *Three television plays* Cape, 1961. op.

OWEN, A. *The wake* in *Theatre choice* ed. by M. Marland, Blackie, 1972.

PLATER, A. *On Christmas Day in the morning* in *You and me* Blackie, 1973.

Radio and television

School broadcasts, both on radio and television, BBC and ITV, provide a wide range of materials that are useful for developing pupils' use of and awareness of language and for encouraging reading. Whenever possible it is best to arrange for programmes to be recorded rather than used off-air, since this provides greater flexibility, allowing you to fit the tape or video-tape into your teaching programme at the most suitable moment. Similarly, it enables you to avoid situations in which large groups of children are crowded together to listen to or to watch programmes. A booklet giving practical advice on how to use educational broadcasts, *School broadcasting: a guide to teachers* by John Lambert, is available from BBC Publications.

Full details of programmes for the academic year are mailed to schools the previous spring. It is important to study them then so that you can order in advance any of the publications that accompany the programmes you want to use. A copy of the teachers' notes, containing details of the programme's contents and suggestions for follow-up work, is essential and enables you to plan how to fit it into your scheme of work. Often there are accompanying pupils' pamphlets which, in the case of series such as *Listening and Writing*, *Speak* and *Books, plays, poems*, provide short anthologies that can be used with the programme, then stored and re-used in subsequent years as source books for thematic work.

It is worth too keeping yourself informed of any serials or films that are shown on television and that are likely to create interest. Children, like adults, enjoy reading books of films or serials that they have enjoyed and Kenneth Cope's *Striker* BBC, 1976, Nina Bawden's *Carrie's war* Gollancz, 1973; Heinemann, 1975; Puffin Books, 1974; David Line's *Run for your life* Cape, 1966; Heinemann, 1975; Puffin Books, 1970 (serialised as *Soldier and me*); Peter Dickinson's *The changes* Gollancz, 1975; and Sylvia Sherry's *A pair of Jesus boots* Cape, 1969; Heinemann, 1975; Puffin Books, 1973 (serialised as *Rocky O'Rourke*) remain popular long after the serialisations have ended.

Radio programmes for 10–13-year-olds
Drama Workshop
Source material for drama classes with 11–13-year-olds. It is advisable to tape record these programmes, to listen to them prior to the session and to refer to the teachers' notes which give suggestions for sectional use.

Inside Pages
For the teacher who looks after the library. A magazine-style programme for 10–12-year-olds with weekly features, such as the story spot and children talking about new books, and other items concerned with the world of books – interviews with authors, on-site recordings, dramatisations and music. Aims to motivate reluctant readers to turn to books for enjoyment and to satisfy the more avid readers by providing plenty of suggestions for further reading.

Listening and Reading I and II
Although these series are designed for younger children (series I for 6 and over, series II for 8 and over) they can be useful with 10- and 11-year-olds who are underachieving readers or slow learners. Each 10-minute broadcast consists of a

complete story and there are pupils' booklets, providing the full text, so that if you record the programmes pupils can listen to the story again and again over a period of time, following the text as they do so.

Listening and Writing

Very useful with 11–14-year-olds for stimulating writing. Provides high quality examples of different kinds of literature. Past series have included plays by Ted Hughes, Ray Jenkins and Alan Ayckbourne, short stories by Walter Macken, Morley Callaghan and George Mackay Brown, serialisations of books such as *Walkabout* and *Old Mali and the boy* and thematic poetry anthologies.

Living Language

Stories and poems for 9–11-year-olds aimed at fostering the individual's creative imagination and to encourage his expression in talk, writing, acting and art. Recent series have included a radiovision programme on Chaucer's pilgrims and versions of *The jungle book* and *The odyssey*, poems by John Walsh and Ian Serraillier and stories by E. L. Konigsberg, Prudence Andrew and George Layton.

Web of Language

A short series of 5 programmes designed to stimulate interest in various aspects of the English language among pupils in the 10–12 age range.

Wordplay: That'd be telling

Designed to encourage spoken language development in children aged 8–12 who are either lacking in confidence or in language ability. Compiled and presented by Michael Rosen the programmes include jokes, riddles, poems, improvised dialogues, songs and stories narrated by people from various regional or cultural communities.

Television programmes for 10–13-year-olds
Over to you

A series on oral English for 10–13-year-olds that can be used to lead on to a wide variety of follow-up activities involving communication.

Writer's Workshop

A wide range of stimulus material aimed at increasing pupils' awareness of language and its possibilities and encouraging them to experiment with words and techniques in their own writing. Presented by the author and poet, Michael Baldwin, the series is designed for 10–13-year-olds, but some programmes are suitable for use with older students as well.

Radio programmes for 14–16-year-olds
Adventure

A series about books for 13–16-year-olds who are able to but reluctant to read. Presents stories in serial form, short stories and extracts from fiction and non-fiction. Programmes on books such as Paula Fox's *The slave dancer*, Clive King's *Me and my million*, Leon Garfield's *Black Jack*, John Rowe Townsend's *Goodnight Prof. Love* and John Steinbeck's *Of mice and men*.

Books, Plays, Poems

Designed to stimulate the enjoyment of works of literature of all sorts and to encourage pupils to write themselves. Includes specially commissioned stories and plays, as well as adaptations of literary masterpieces such as *Don Quixote* and *The turn of the screw* and radio anthologies of poems by contemporary poets, on themes or from a particular period. For 14–17-year-olds.

Speak

A series of spoken English programmes for 14–16-year-olds. Presents a wide range of material designed to promote discussion. Authors and contributors to recent series include Alan

Bennett, Lesley Davies, Barrie Keefe, Peter Porter, Carl Sandburg and Zulfikar Ghose.

Television programmes for 14–16-year-olds
English
Presents two plays relevant to the needs and interests of pupils from 14 to 17, usually chosen from the recommended lists for GCE and CSE examinations. Recent productions have been *A taste of honey, Heil Caesar!, Zigger zagger* and *The government inspector*. Future series will feature Sean O'Casey's *The plough and the stars* and Willis Hall's *The long and the short and the tall*. The plays are accompanied by documentary programmes on literature and writing.

The English Programme
Provides material designed to support work in English for the 13–18 age range. Includes units on TV drama, mass communications in society, a Shakespeare play, language and on a theme presented through a number of documentaries.

Looking at television
A series aimed to encourage pupils to look more critically at television, to question some of the views that are expressed on TV and to exercise some choice in their viewing habits. Written and presented by Peter Fiddick, television critic of *The Guardian*.

The Messengers
Extracts from features and documentary films and from television programmes chosen to provide discussion material around themes. Particularly useful if you run a communications or media studies option course.

Scene
Documentary programmes and specially commissioned plays on contemporary issues, designed to stimulate thought, discussion and classwork of various kinds. An excellent series, particularly useful with less motivated pupils.

Subjects covered include crime and punishment, teenage magazines, violence and young marriage. Among the playwrights who have contributed to the series are Peter Terson, Colin Welland and Alan Plater.

Starting Out
A 10-part serial story by Catherine Storr, most suitable for use with less motivated, under-achieving students. Designed to help adolescents understand and cope with the challenges which face them as they prepare to take their places in the adult world, it can be used in conjunction with *Who's Bill?*, a novel by Catherine Storr, based on the series and available as a Macmillan Topliner, 1977.

Local and regional programmes
Each of the 20 BBC local radio stations has an education producer and together they transmit about 120 series per term for schools, a number of which are designed to promote language development. You can get full details from your local radio station.

There are also a number of radio and television programmes broadcast only in Scotland or Northern Ireland. Currently, for example, there is the television programme, *Time to Think*, designed to appeal directly to teaching of the English 'O' Grade Paper 1B – Reading.

Finding out about resources
Keeping up to date with the resources that are available is not easy even for the most dedicated and enthusiastic teacher. But it is important to do so, for the success or failure of your lesson often depends to a large extent on the material that you use. It is worth remembering too that your whole approach to a particular topic may be determined by whatever resources are available.

Mistakes can be expensive and you have to live with them, so always take a detailed look at a range of books or materials before deciding what to buy. Here are some ways that you can keep in touch.

Publishers' catalogues

Publishers regularly mail catalogues to schools, giving full details of their publications, and are usually willing to send teachers inspection copies on request. The catalogues are arranged according to subject and, in the secondary school, are often addressed to the head of department. Unfortunately in many schools he is the only person to see them and merely gives them a cursory glance before adding them to an unsorted pile in a drawer or locker. Ideally they should be studied to see if there is anything worth sending for on inspection and then filed systematically in alphabetical order in a filing cabinet. If no filing cabinet is available, then they can be stored in a cardboard box and pieces of card used to mark the alphabetic divisions. Whichever method is used, it means that the catalogues are made accessible to all the members of a department and it also makes it easier for the head of department himself, whenever he wants to find a reference to enable him to order a book.

Some of the publishers' handouts, such as the recent *Knockouts* leaflet, make attractive posters for the library or classroom walls, and can be used to keep pupils informed of new titles. Others like the *Topliner* and *Getaway* catalogues, with their colourful reproductions of covers, the *Puffin* and the *New Windmill* catalogue, *What shall they read?*, containing illustrations as well as brief descriptions of the books, can be cut up and pasted on to card to make book cards, for use in the library lesson, providing both teacher and pupils with a checklist of titles available on, for example, a particular theme.

As well as the Puffin catalogue, and *Puffin*

post, which is mailed to members of the Puffin Club, Penguin have also produced a very useful booklet, *Penguins in schools: a guide for teachers*, suggesting ways in which books from the Puffin and Peacock series can be integrated into theme and topic work. It is available from Penguin Books Ltd.

Reviews

The *Times Educational Supplement* has a reviews section each week, which includes middle-school and secondary-school books. Three times a year

there is a children's book supplement and periodically there are insets focussing on different areas of the curriculum in which new resources are reviewed and new approaches discussed.

The *Times Literary Supplement* reviews recent fiction and non-fiction for children quarterly in a children's book supplement, which can be subscribed to independently. Details are available from Times Newspapers Ltd. There is also a monthly *Reviewsheet*, dealing with new fiction for nine- to sixteen-year-olds. Books are judged primarily on how much they will appeal to children. Started by two Sheffield school-teachers, Steve Bowles and Jane Powell, it is available from Jane Powell, Sydenham School, Dartmouth Road, London SE26. Another booklet of reviews, *Growing point* (nine issues a year) can be obtained from Margery Fisher, Ashton Manor, Northampton NN7 2JL.

Teachers' centres and reading centres

There are several hundred teachers' centres in various parts of the country. Many of them have very good reading resource areas and are well worth a visit. Some authorities and colleges of education have also set up reading centres offering specialist advice on language and reading. One that deserves particular mention is the Centre for the Teaching of Reading at the University of Reading. There is a permanent exhibition of reading materials for all age groups, including a separate display of books suitable for use with older teenagers and adult non-readers. The display is open to everyone, not just professionals who live in the area. In addition the Centre publishes a number of inexpensive booklets and tape-recorded short talks by experts such as David Crystal, and offers a postal and telephone information service. Details of its publications can be obtained from Betty Root, Tutor-in-charge, Centre for the Teaching of Reading, University of Reading School of Education, 29 Eastern Avenue, Reading, Berkshire RG1 5RU.

National Association for the Teaching of English

Over the past decade this organisation has played a major part in disseminating ideas concerning all aspects of language development and in particular in making teachers aware of the need to develop a language policy across the curriculum. Its journal, *English in education*, published three times a year, contains articles on language theory and all aspects of English in the classroom, often of significance to teachers of every subject, not just English. A working party of its members has produced the useful pamphlet, *Language across the curriculum, guidelines for schools*, written by Mike Torbe and published by Ward Lock Educational. There is an annual course conference at Easter. In 1977 one of the commissions, chaired by Iris Leyland, organised in conjunction with COSTA (the Committee of Subject Teachers Associations), discussed language across the curriculum, considering the implications of Chapter 12 of the Bullock report. Details of membership from NATE office, Fernleigh, 10B Thornhill Road, Edgerton, Huddersfield HD3 3AU.

Centre for Information on the Teaching of English

Situated at the Moray House College of Education in Edinburgh, CITE acts as the focal point for curriculum development and support in English teaching in Scotland. It has a large library of books of concern to teachers of English, including textbooks, which is open daily and books can be borrowed by post. It also publishes the magazine *Teaching English* (three issues a year), which contains reviews as well as articles. The October 1976 issue contained an article on *Encouraging effective reading* by Colin Harrison in which he wrote about 'silent reading with group discussion' activities and their effectiveness. The Spring 1977 edition contained papers on language, including a description of an experimental post-graduate course, *Language Across the Curriculum* by Mary Karus and Sister Valerio, and an article on *A whole school language policy* by Patrick J. McLaughlin. Subscription details from CITE, Moray House College of Education, Holyrood Road, Edinburgh EH8 8AQ.

National Association of Remedial Education

This organisation concerns itself with all aspects of remedial education and issues a number of publications, which teachers of slow learners and underachieving readers in the secondary school may find useful. Among them are *The A–Z of reading*, a book listing several hundred books, which gives an assessment of the readability level based on the Spache Readability Test and contains a section on secondary titles for slower learners; and *A classroom index of phonic resources*, giving details of resources available for helping with the teaching of phonic skills. Details of publications and membership from NARE, 4 Old Croft Road, Walton-on-the-Hill, Stafford.

The School Library Association

This association concerns itself with all aspects of the organisation of books and resources within schools and has many local branches, which organise courses and talks. It publishes the magazine *School Librarian* (quarterly), which contains articles on books, libraries and authors as well as several pages of reviews. Details of membership from School Library Association, Victoria House, 29–31 George Street, Oxford OX1 2AY.

The Schools Council

The Schools Council has funded research projects into various aspects of language and reading including the development of writing abilities, oracy, children's reading habits, writing across the curriculum and the effective use of reading. Details of current projects and of Schools Council publications from the Information section, Schools Council, Great Portland Street, London W1N 8LL.

Four booklists

Individualised reading Cliff Moon. Centre for the Teaching of Reading, 7th rev. edn 1977.
Comparative lists of selected books for young readers. Books have been chosen specifically with an interest level below the 11-year age group and are not, therefore, always appropriate for use with older pupils.

Retarded and reluctant readers Bridie Raban and Wendy Body. Centre for the Teaching of Reading, 1976.
Graded lists of selected books for secondary school pupils. Books are categorised within 12 stages, according to the approximate reading age required to read them.

Help in reading Stanley S. Segal and Tom Pascoe. National Book League, 6th edn 1975.

An annotated list of books for the slow learner and underachieving reader.

Starting point Betty Root and Sue Brownhill. National Book League, 1975.
An annotated list of books for the illiterate adult and older reluctant reader.

What happens to the publishers' catalogues that are sent to your school?

Does your school subscribe to any of the journals or organisations mentioned in this section?

Is there a local branch of either the National Association for the Teaching of English or the School Library Association in your area?

Is there a teachers' centre or reading centre in your area? What advice on reading and language does it offer?

Part 5   An Annotated bibliography

by John L. Foster

The following list describes the books that I have found most useful in helping me to formulate and refine my ideas about language and reading and to develop my classroom practices. It includes a number of books on oracy, drama and writing, as well as on language development, reading and remedial reading. No list can hope to be exhaustive. Details of other books that you might find useful are often given in the bibliographies that the recommended books themselves contain. There are several extremely useful American texts, but I have omitted them on the grounds that they can be very difficult to obtain.

BARNES, D. *From communication to curriculum* Penguin Books, 1976. An examination of how children use speech in the course of learning and of how the patterns of classroom communication affect learning. It puts forward the view that some children fail in school because traditional teaching practice restricts their development, rather than because they have difficulty with language. A book that provides food for thought not only about classroom practice but about our whole approach to the curriculum.

BARNES, D. et al. *Language, the learner and the school* Penguin Books, 1969. An Open University set book, consisting of Douglas Barnes's 'Language in the secondary classroom', a study of language interaction in 12 lessons in the first term of secondary education; an article by James Britton, 'Talking to learn', on the function of talk in the development of thought and a discussion document, prepared by Harold Rosen, on behalf of the London Association for the Teaching of English, 'Towards a language policy across the curriculum'. A valuable book for teachers of children of all ages, particularly Douglas Barnes's survey, which includes an analysis of teachers' questions, pupils' participation and the language of instruction, revealing

the effect and significance of the classroom language that teachers use and expect.

BURGESS, T. et al. *Understanding children writing* Penguin Books, 1973. An anthology of all kinds of writing prepared by a group of 10 teachers with an introduction and linking commentary, designed to draw the reader into the world of the child as he writes. Provides insights into the difficulties and excitements of the child's situation and into what is involved in the different writing tasks that teachers set pupils.

CALTHROP, K. *Reading together* Heinemann, 1971; n.e. paperback 1973. An investigation into the use of the class reader, examining teachers' theories of its value, their criteria for their choice of books and giving an account of the ways in which class readers were being used by a number of teachers in the late 1960s. An interesting survey of attitudes and practices that is well worth consulting if you are in doubt about whether to use a class reader, what to choose or how you might develop work on it.

CASHDAN, A. and GRUGEON, E. eds. *Language in education* Routledge and Kegan Paul, 1972. A sourcebook of readings, designed for the use of Open University students following the Language and Learning course. Interesting papers on all aspects of language in the educational context. Section 4 – Language in the classroom – is the most significant for middle and secondary school teachers containing articles by Douglas Barnes on 'Language and learning in the classroom' and Harold Rosen's 'The language of textbooks'.

CHAMBERS, A. *The reluctant reader* Pergamon Press, 1969, o.p. Explores the reasons why teenagers, who can read, may in their adolescent years become reluctant readers and makes out a case for the provision of books specifically designed to capture their interest and meet their needs. A clear statement of his position from Aidan Chambers, the general editor of the *Topliner*, *Club 75* and *Rockets* series.

CHAMBERS, A. *Introducing books to children* Heinemann Educational, 1973. A book for students and young teachers in which the author sets out the reasons why he considers literary reading above all is important to everyone, and gives practical advice on how to encourage children to read voraciously. There are sections on how to arrange the right setting for reading, the need to plan story-telling and the value of reading aloud, the organisation of book-related activities, the use of the library, setting up a school bookshop and inviting authors to talk with children about their books.

CREBER, J. W. P. *Lost for words* Penguin Books, 1971. Commissioned by the National Association for the Teaching of English as a consequence of an international seminar on 'The Language of failure'. Argues that the child from a culturally and linguistically deprived home starts with a severe handicap and that his failure is compounded by the restricted opportunities for language development in schools. Examines a wide range of classroom situations and urges the need for a greater emphasis on language and on the social learning that accompanies it.

DEPARTMENT OF EDUCATION AND SCIENCE *A language for life*: Report of the Committee of Inquiry appointed by the Secretary of State for Education and Science under the chairmanship of Sir Alan Bullock. Her Majesty's Stationery Office, 1975.
Part 2, Ch. 4 Language and learning; Part 3, Ch. 6 The reading process, Ch. 8 Reading, the later stages, Ch. 9 Literature; all of Part 4 – Language in the middle and secondary years – Ch. 10 Oral language, Ch. 11 Written language, Ch. 12 Language across the curriculum; Part 5 – Organisation – Ch. 14 Continuity between schools, Ch. 15 The secondary school; Part 6, Ch. 18 Children with reading difficulties; Part 7 – Resources – Ch. 21 Books, Ch. 22 Technological aids and broadcasting.

DIXON, J. *Growth through English: set in the perspective of the seventies* Oxford University Press, 3rd rev. edn 1975. A report based on an Anglo-American conference on the teaching of English (the Dartmouth seminar) held in 1966, published by the National Association for the Teaching of English on behalf of NATE, the National Council of Teachers of English and the Modern Language Association of America. A book that was extremely influential in spreading new attitudes towards English in the late 1960s and that is important to the student teacher of English as a statement of the philosophy behind, and the implications of, the 'personal growth' model of English teaching. The new edition contains an additional chapter setting the book in the perspective of the 1970s.

DOUGHTY, P. S. et al. *Language in use* Edward Arnold, 1971. The Schools Council programme in linguistics and English teaching. A loose-leaf folder consisting of 110 units, each of which provides an outline for a sequence of lessons, aimed at developing an awareness of what language is and how it is used. A valuable sourcebook of ideas which can be adapted to fit into your own programme according to the particular needs of your situation.

FADER, D. *Hooked on books* Pergamon Press, 1969, o.p. An account of how the author set about encouraging juvenile delinquents in an American training school to read and of how they became 'hooked on books'. Examines the reasons why youngsters may often be reluctant readers and convincingly argues for an approach to reading in schools and colleges that involves the use of popular magazines and newspapers and the widest possible variety of paperback books.

FOSTER, J. L. ed. *Reluctant to read?* Ward Lock, 1977. A collection of articles which consider the philosophy that lies behind a policy of tackling the problem of reluctance by making a special provision for such readers, re-examine the nature and causes of reluctance to read and give details of titles and of approaches that have proved successful in the classroom. Contributors include Geoff Fox, Robert Leeson and Sheila Ray.

FOX, G. et al. eds. *Writers, critics and children* Heinemann Educational, 1976. A collection of articles which first appeared in the journal, *Children's literature in education.* In Part 1 writers such as Nina Bawden, Joan Aiken and Geoffrey Trease consider some of the challenges and choices implicit in writing for children. Part 2 is concerned with evaluation and critical discussion of children's fiction and includes Ted Hughes on 'Myth and education' and 'A defence of rubbish' by Peter Dickinson. Part 3 focusses on the young readers themselves and on the use of literature in schools. Among the contributions are a discussion of 'How children respond to fiction' by Nicholas Tucker and a description of a school policy for readers of all abilities by John Foster.

GILLILAND, J. and MERRITT, J. *Readability* University of London Press, 1972. A teaching of reading monograph, produced in collaboration with the United Kingdom Reading Association, providing an introduction to the subject of readability. Discusses the concept of readability and explains the major considerations, which are involved in matching particular books to particular readers. Aspects of book production, such as typography and format, are discussed and methods of assessing readability are

described. It has a useful selected annotated bibliography for anyone interested in further studying the question of readability.

HOLLINDALE, P. *Choosing books for children* Paul Elek, 1974. Deals with the selection of books for those children who do not experience reading difficulties or show a reluctance to read. A helpful guide for parents and teachers, which suggests a set of criteria that can be applied to any book and discusses a wide range of titles. Chapters 5–8 are concerned with books for 10–16-year-olds.

KOHL, H. *Reading, how to* Penguin Books, 1974. A book that sets out to destroy some of the myths that surround the teaching of reading and argues that anyone who can read with a certain degree of competency can help others who read less well, provided that the learning situation is an open, caring and informal one. Offers numerous suggestions for developing reading programmes and creating reading materials out of the artefacts of the learner's world. Particularly useful as a sourcebook of ideas for use with older secondary pupils, who have failed to learn to read.

LAWRENCE D. *Improved reading through counselling* Ward Lock, 1973, o.p. Focusses on the emotional factor that may lie behind reading failure and describes experiments which showed that it is possible to improve a child's self-image and ultimately his reading attainment by a systematic counselling approach. The second part offers helpful suggestions of ways to set up a counselling programme.

LYNSKEY, A. M. *Children and themes* Oxford University Press, 1974. A practical guide describing ways of widening the experience of pupils in the middle-school age range by a thematic approach through drama and literature. The first section sets out a theoretical framework for such an approach, while the second focusses on 16 themes, provides detailed ideas for drama work and shows how it can be linked to literature and writing. A handbook of valuable suggestions that any teacher of 9–13-year-olds can readily adapt to suit his own particular situation.

MARLAND, M. ed. *Language across the curriculum* Heinemann Educational, 1977. Edited by Michael Marland, a member of the Bullock Committee, this book explores the implications of the Bullock report for every department in the secondary school. There are specialist contributions from Nancy Martin, Douglas Barnes, Keith Gardner, Colin Harrison and others. Together the authors put forward a coherent plan for the development of a language policy in every curriculum area.

MARTIN, N. et al. *Understanding children talking* Penguin Books, 1976. A book which arose from the work of some members of the London Association for the Teaching of English. It explores children's use of language by presenting transcripts of children talking in a variety of situations both in and out of school. Chapter 4, 'Work talk in school', with examples of a mathematics lesson, of groups discussing a poem with and without a teacher, and of talk while on a geography field trip is particularly illuminating.

MARTIN, N. et al. *Writing and learning across the curriculum* Ward Lock, 1976. Compiled by the Schools Council Writing across the Curriculum Project Team. Discusses the central part that writing and talking play in the learning process and suggests that too much writing and talking in school is used to test what children know and that too little is concerned with enabling them to make sense of things for themselves. Using examples of children's writing the book examines the range of writing, talking and audiences that can be made available to children and what

happens when they take up these opportunities.

MERRITT, J. and MELNIK, A. eds. *Reading: today and tomorrow* Hodder and Stoughton, 1972. One of the textbooks produced for the Open University course on Reading Development, consisting of material drawn from papers published in academic journals, conference proceedings and extracts from books on reading. Part 1 – What is reading? contains articles on the nature of the reading process, the nature and influence of the media and the developing abilities of the reader. Part 2 – Present standards and future needs surveys the state of reading, current provision and future needs.

MERRITT, J. and MELNIK, A. eds. *The reading curriculum* Hodder and Stoughton, 1972. A companion volume to *Reading: today and tomorrow*. Part 1 sections A and B on the place of reading in the curriculum, Part 2 sections C and D on comprehension skills and vocabulary development, Part 3 section B on classroom techniques of asking questions and Part 4 section A on the assessment of readability of printed media would probably be the most useful to middle school and secondary school teachers.

MOON, C. and RABAN, B. *A question of reading* Ward Lock, 1975. Although this deals with the organisation of resources for reading in primary schools, it is also a useful book for middle and secondary school teachers, describing the reading process, the needs and abilities of children and what books should provide for the reader. Much of the sound practical advice on how to match children and reading materials and how to organise the reading class can be adapted for, and extended into, the middle and secondary school classroom.

REID, J. F. ed. *Reading: problems and practices* Ward Lock, 1972. Consists of papers from America and Britain providing a guide to basic factors involved in reading difficulties. Useful to anyone dealing with slow learners and non-readers, particularly section 3 on specific reading difficulties and section 4 on diagnosis and remedial treatment.

SCHER, A. and VERRALL, C. *100 + ideas for drama* Heinemann Educational, 1975. A compendium of drama activities that can be developed with children of all ages, compiled by the directors of the Anna Scher Children's Theatre in Islington. Provides a fund of tried and tested ideas that you can delve into whenever you are at a loss as to what to do in your next drama lesson.

SELF, D. *A practical guide to drama in the secondary school* Ward Lock, 1975. A sourcebook of ideas for creative drama lessons for use at all levels of the secondary school, ranging from suggestions for movement lessons and verbal improvisations to others on playmaking and documentary work. There are useful sections on how to plan not only the immediate lesson, but the whole term's work, and an interesting chapter 'Towards performance', arguing the case for 'showing' creative work to carefully selected audiences.

SELF, D. *Talk: a practical guide to oral work in the secondary school* Ward Lock, 1976. A practical handbook of advice on how to organise and develop talk as a purposeful classroom activity. Offers guidance on classroom management, control and follow-up activities, as well as numerous ideas for oral work of all kinds.

STRATTA, L. et al. *Patterns of language* Heinemann Educational, 1973. Concerns itself with all aspects of the teaching of English. Chapter 2, 'Literature and interpretation', is particularly valuable, stressing the close relationship between interpretative and creative activities and giving examples of how texts may be explored creatively.

TANSLEY, A. E. *Reading and remedial reading* Routledge and Kegan Paul, 1967, n.e. paperback 1972. A book for the remedial specialist, describing the reading programme that the author developed in a school for educationally subnormal/maladjusted pupils and the diagnosis and treatment of acute difficulties in learning to read. Many of the methods and techniques can be applied to all children who are experiencing difficulty in learning to read. Chapters 8, 9 and 10 particularly.

TORBE, M. and PROTHEROUGH, R. eds. *Classroom encounters* Ward Lock, 1976. A collection of articles on the theme of language and English teaching which first appeared in the National Association for the Teaching of English journal, *English in education*. The editors' introduction gives a clear and concise summary of the changes that have taken place in English teaching in the last 15 years and of the importance of recent developments in language theory. The articles themselves explore the principles underlying these changes and how they can be put into practice. Many of them, such as Margaret Mallet's article on middle school project/topic work and Paul Williams's 'Talk and discussion' – an examination of the transcripts of lessons in several subjects – argue for providing more opportunity for talk in small groups.

WALKER, C. *Reading development and extension* Ward Lock, 1974. Offers advice on how to extend the skills of children who can already read. Gives help on how to draw up a set of reading goals and suggests teaching techniques and an organisational framework for achieving them. A very practical book outlining ways that you can ensure that children learn to read critically, efficiently and habitually, both for information and for enjoyment.

WHITEHEAD, F. et al. *Children's reading interests*

(Schools Council, Working Paper 52) Evans/
Methuen, 1974. The interim report from the
Schools Council research project into children's
reading habits 10–15, directed by Frank
Whitehead. More important for the significant
points that are made about the provision and
selection of books in the Discussion section than
for the account of the research findings – the
result of a 1971 survey.

WILKINSON, A. M. *The foundations of language:
talking and reading in young children* Oxford
University Press, 1971. A very clear account of
modern linguistic theory, of how language is
acquired and how it relates to thought. The final
chapters deal with the beginnings of reading,
describing various methods and approaches. A
useful introduction to the study of language
and reading for teachers of children of all ages.

WILKINSON, A. M. *Language and education*
Oxford University Press, 1975. Begins with a
discussion of different types of communication
both verbal and non-verbal, going on to consider
the various aspects of language, the functions of
language and its relationship to thought. The
importance of language in learning is then
explored. The second part is designed as a workbook and consists of examples which provide a
basis for further work on the subject.

WILKINSON, A. M. et al. *The quality of listening*
Macmillan, 1974. The report of the Schools
Council Oracy Project 11–18. An important
book, because while there has been a great deal
of research recently into reading, writing and
talking, there has been little study of the activity
of listening. The authors analyse features of
spoken language such as tone, meaning, the
demands of context and the variations caused by
different social and occupational environments.
Of particular interest is Chapter 5 which suggests
reasons for poor listening and indicates some

ways in which the study of spoken language
might be undertaken in the classroom.

WOLFF, S. *Children under stress* Penguin, 1973.
An examination of emotional disturbance in one-
parent children, orphans, children in hospital and
children otherwise deprived. Useful to the teacher
of reading as a reminder of the stress which
children can be suffering and which often is one
of the underlying causes of reading failure.

BARNES, D. et al. *Language, the learner and the school* Penguin 1969.

BARNES, D. *From communication to curriculum* Penguin, 1976.

BRITTON, J. *Language and learning* Allen Lane/Penguin, 1970.

BURGESS, C. et al. *Understanding children writing* Penguin, 1973.

CLAY, M. M. *Reading: the patterning of complex behaviour* Heinemann Educational, 1973.

FLANDERS, N. *Analysing teaching behaviour* Addison-Wesley, 1970.

GOODMAN, K. ed. *Miscue analysis: applications to reading instruction* (ERIC Clearing House on Reading and Communication Skills) campaign III: National Council of Teachers of English, 1973.

JONES, A. and MULFORD, J. (eds.) *Children using language* Oxford, 1971.

MARTIN, N. et al. *Writing and learning across the curriculum* Ward Lock, 1976.

WILKINSON, A. *Language and education* Oxford, 1975.

Index